OUR
STORIES
OUR LIVES

EDITED BY WAHIDA SHAFFI

This edition published in Great Britain in 2009 by The Policy Press for the
Joseph Rowntree Foundation

The Policy Press
University of Bristol
Fourth Floor
Beacon House
Queen's Road
Bristol BS8 1QU, UK

Tel +44 (0)117 331 4054
Fax +44 (0)117 331 4093
e-mail tpp-info@bristol.ac.uk
www.policypress.org.uk

North American office:
The Policy Press
c/o International Specialized Books Services
920 NE 58th Avenue, Suite 300
Portland, OR 97213-3786, USA
Tel +1 503 287 3093
Fax +1 503 280 8832
e-mail info@isbs.com

CONTENTS

Thank You   4

Today's World   7

Glossary   11

ARSHAD BEGUM AJEEB   *The Mayoress*   15

FATIMA AYUB   *The Pioneer*   21

BARKAT BIBI   *Dadi Ma the Motivator*   27

NASREEN CHOUDHURY   *From Sylhet to Ilkley*   33

ELANA DAVIS   *Music 'n' Motherhood*   41

NATASHA ALMAS FELL   *Identity*   47

SENSEI MUMTAZ KHAN   *No Mercy!*   51

NEGARA KHATUN   *Journey to the House of Allah*   59

REJWANA MALIK   *I Have a Dream!*   67

SOFIA MASKIN   *From Roots to Routes*   73

SYIMA MERALI   *Jihad*   79

UMM MOHSIN   *The Preacher's Voice*   87

SHAHANA RAHMAN   *Salaam Namaste*   93

ZOHRA J RASHID   *The Visionary*   99

ZEHIDA REHMAN   *Turning Pennies into Pounds*   107

ULFAT RIAZ   *Busing In the Immigrants*   113

AKHTAR SHEIKH   *White Abbey Road*   121

RINA (RADHIA) TARAFDER   *The Spiritual Tourist*   127

SELINA ULLAH   *Burning Ambitions*   133

JEAN (RABIA) YOUSFI   *Rags to Riches*   139

Final Thoughts   145

THANK YOU

Life has blessed me with many guiding influences – each in their own way contributing to the process leading up to this book. This book was born out of a vision exploring the insights and experiences of Muslim women in Bradford and has relied heavily on the support and encouragement of many friends and colleagues. Despite the uplifting nature of the past few years, they have not been without the occasional challenge and, were it not for the unseen hands that continuously reach out to inspire and support and prove to be a source of great power and wisdom, the project would have been a daunting prospect. However, what proves even more challenging is trying to find the appropriate words to show my gratitude and in turn do justice to the scores of individuals who have embraced this project and have worked tirelessly in various ways. They say gratitude is often far more than simply saying 'thank you', it is truly appreciating the people, experiences, blessings and circumstances that create an existence unique to you. Therefore the process has been very much about interdependence and reliance not only on the women who have participated in/and are featured in the book audio conversational recordings, website, seminars and films – but also, those men and women who have extended their hands with heartfelt consideration without expecting anything in return.

First and foremost I want to thank the 20 women who have chosen to contribute their stories and in doing so open up their lives to others. Over the years I have felt profoundly moved and privileged by women's stories, opinions and experiences and their ability to offer incredible insights with an honesty and openness that warrants respect. I pray that we have managed to capture their voices through the various mediums in a way that does justice to the passionate and courageous ways in which their words have been expressed.

Second, I would like to acknowledge the WWTE OurLives Team who have over the years helped to breathe life into my vision; working above and beyond their capacity and allotted times; and becoming respected loyal friends in the process. Beginning with Nuzhat Ali (project worker), who has been an anchor of support and guidance. For years she has been a constant source of inspiration to me; her sheer hard work and dedication despite home schooling her children, illness and other work commitments is applauded. Nick Francis of Speak-It Productions for providing the organisational support and overseeing all the film aspects of the project. He has had to put up with my very long emails, texts, production schedules and endless queries and has patiently helped me to grow in my understanding of documentary film making. Shanaz Gulzar, Participatory Film Coordinator, whose energy and commitment to encouraging learning about film was unwavering; providing humour and openness in abundance. Clive Edwin Collier for his brotherly advice and assistance with the documentary films and in particular for his work on the Making of Film. Sasha Bhatt of Dar al Sasha for her commitment and work on the initial design phase of the website; ensuring that in time the vision would be made accessible to the globe online and act as a vehicle to mobilise women around the world. Amra Ejaz, our passionate and skilled book photographer and finally, Irna Qureshi, who has played a vital role by bringing her expertise in the field of oral history to aide the telling of the women's stories in the book from selection through to narrative formation. Needless to say, any failings rest with me alone.

From the Joseph Rowntree Foundation my special thanks extend to Bana Gora. Regardless of the incessant and at times intense discussions that have surfaced during various points, we were allowed to maintain our sense of independence throughout the course of this project – a luxury that can often be thwarted in such relationships. She has consistently been a pillar of support and has always played a proactive role in encouraging and offering genuine assistance where appropriate. I am also thankful to Rosemary Knowles (Publishing Manager, JRF) for opening up the space for the creation of a more creative publication – in such a short period of time. The Policy Press for overseeing the publication and offering constructive editorial inputs and Ali Shaw (Director of The Policy Press) in particular for her understanding, sensitivity and patience throughout the design and production phases. Members of the Advisory Group who continue to be committed, vocal and passionate as well as individuals at the University of Bradford, who have shown their support in many practical ways.

Others deserving of my acknowledgement and appreciation include Peter and Margaret Maddison, my friends whose letters and gifts have never failed to make me smile. Also Zulfiqar Ahmed and Pranav Patel for providing advice, humour, constructive and forthright insights, and for gently encouraging me to look beyond my narrow scope. Majad Ali Fazil, my trusted friend and confidant for all of his support, encouragement, written words and conversations – all of which are and always will be appreciated. And many more who have sincerely cared in quieter, more prayerful ways. Last but by no means least, my precious family, especially my sisters Zahida, Sajida and Taheera who have gently picked me up and made me smile when I have fallen on numerous occasions since 2003, without judgement and with genuine care. They have offered constructive advice, the comfort of their arms and have always had the confidence and faith in my abilities, choices, internal worth and strength of character. My sister-in-law, Shahida, who has received very little help with the housework over the years but has never complained. And most of all my parents, who have had to patiently put up with my late nights, lack of communication and absenteeism but who have continuously prayed for my wellbeing and have always encouraged me to strive hard and give of myself.

Wahida Shaffi

TODAY'S WORLD

In the opening years of the 21st century, I see a number of Muslim women who have achieved positions of influence – in local government, business, further and higher education, charities and other organisations. Women who care about the society in which they live and bring up their children; women who increasingly find a voice together to promote values and who work together to make things happen. There's a considerable way to go in harnessing the potential that lies at the heart of this change and there is a need to acknowledge that there also continues to be a disproportionate lack of reflection on women's achievements and experiences. But there is plenty of evidence to suggest that Muslim women are paving the way forward in new dynamic, challenging and creative ways. This book is all about them, women of multiple generations who do not see themselves as victims. They depict the courage, dignity and strength of women who have embraced life in all its endless variety. Pioneers, who have recognised their potential in the public and private realms of society; who have struggled, made sacrifices and both intellectually and critically challenged themselves, conventional norms and strategic governmental policies. They have taken pride in their multiple and changing identities and are committed to positive and peaceful change. Therefore these stories will resonate with women around the world and not just the UK by virtue of the universalism of human values and the innate struggle to better ourselves and society in modern times and for future generations.

It all began as a vision designed to explore the insights and experiences of Muslim women in Bradford. It focused on over a hundred women, from the ages of 14 to 80 of all walks of life – and harnessed media technologies to capture their insights. The aim was to empower women to present themselves in their own words through participatory video, documentary film, audio, oral history/narratives and the internet. A series of inspiring change seminars and conferences was also organised to enable women to engage with issues of importance to them and in turn inspire debate and action. The result is a number of engaging cameos that identify their hopes, aspirations and concerns through their day-to-day activities. Throughout the process of producing the videos and other media material, their voices remained pivotal, unobscured by over-much analysis and interpretation.

This book focuses on just 20 of the women; each one has played a central role in the formation of their own story and allows us to go into more depth. But before we turn to their narratives, it is important to offer a context within which these stories and wider conversations with women were gathered.

Half a billion of the world's population are Muslim women and Muslims are the second largest faith-based community in the UK; making up 3% of the population. Bradford is home to one of the largest Muslim communities in the UK. It is often cited as a place of complexity and conflict with particular reference to its ethnic make-up. Historically Bradford used to be one of the wealthiest towns of early industrial England, and although its business heart is still strong, as with most post-industrial cities, it has been vulnerable to changing market patterns, foreign competition, cheaper low-cost locations and a shrinking manufacturing base. One important factor throughout its history has been immigration, which has played a strong part in life of the city, bringing a rich diversity of influences from the Eastern European, Irish, German and Jewish communities. It has been argued that it was the cheap labour provided by these immigrant communities that kept the textile industries alive and kicking in recent decades. Now many of the newcomers are from Eastern and Central Europe; before them, the labour force came from the Asian subcontinent, and it is the South Asian and African Caribbean presence that is often the focus of any definition of the city, making Bradford the subject of curious eyes and numerous reports. And there has been many a challenging episode in its recent history. Despite this, Bradford has much more to offer than the frequently negative depictions. And for many of the women in the book it continues to be a city to which they feel proud to belong.

Global events have also shaped the experience of Muslims in Britain. The War in Gaza (Palestine) in 2009 has seen numerous protests around the world's capitals. The sight of planes flying into the Twin Towers in New York on September 11th 2001 will remain an iconic image that changed the way Muslims were viewed – not only in their own neighbourhoods but also around the world. The years following saw the 'war on terror' and military interventions in Iraq despite large-scale protests from all segments of British society. Such US and UK foreign policy served only to further alienate large sections of the Muslim community in the UK. The 7/7 attacks on the London transport system in 2005 fuelled communal tensions. Many human rights groups recorded an increase in racist and Islamophobic attitudes. Despite the clear message of prominent faith leaders that Islam was not an enemy of the West and that a few misguided individuals should not tarnish the reputation of an entire group, growing polarisations between Islam and the West continued to be assumed by the press and concerns of 'home-grown terrorism' escalated. Recent history has demonstrated that wealthier Western democracies can no longer isolate themselves from events taking place elsewhere in the world; and many eagerly wait to see whether the election of Barack Hussein Obama will result in a paradigm shift. We live in an increasingly interconnected and interdependent world where different religions and ethnic communities need to learn about each other in order to live in peace. As Archbishop Desmond Tutu rightly said, "The real threat to global peace lies in our failure to recognise our interdependence". This is no longer an option but a necessity.

At home, current debates have focused on whether the term 'multiculturalism' has served its time, following the reports of Cantle (2001), Denham (2001) and Ouseley (2005), which all stressed the importance of 'community cohesion', a perceived remedy for divisions in our society. In the midst of all these dramatic events, Muslim women in Britain began to take centre stage – with the veil becoming a symbol for political debates on integration, cohesion and radicalisation. Much of this coverage portrayed Muslim women as the subjugated victims of oppressive patriarchal cultures, with a widespread assumption that they are one large homogeneous group. In fact there are a large variety of Muslim women around the world, from the vastly different cultures of the Middle East, South East Asia, South Asia, Yugoslavia, Northern Africa and the Southern parts of the former USSR. And the experiences of women in each of these countries, is unique to them – just as it is for women in the UK or US.

Over the past few decades the UK has seen major demographic, social and cultural changes. Muslims have emerged at the heart of countless critical debates and analysis with particular reference to mainland and global security, cohesion, participation and integration, marriage, immigration and also educational and economic disadvantage. Many of these debates have continued to homogenise Muslim men and women, and failed to represent the rich diversity of opinion within Islam and between people. There has also been a failure to make space and respect the views, experiences and insights of young people and women; and both groups are vital in any meaningful discussions that explore the ingredients for positive social change. When they are heard, the result is the evolution of alternative, fresh and more dynamic responses and spaces that enrich current debates and offer alternative insights.

The OurLives Project emerged out of the desire to foreground Muslim women's voices and experiences into the debates developing against the backdrop of events that were unfolding in Britain. The project flourished through conversations with other like-minded women, Muslim and non-Muslim, who understood the importance of creativity and the need for alternative ways to recognise and celebrate the contribution that Muslim women can and do make and the challenges they face. The stories told here emphasise the power of people's lives and in turn provide a framework to aid deeper debate and understanding and encourage a culture of critical openness. Using stories and narrative as a central tool, this book belongs within a long tradition where lessons, history and practical knowledge have been passed from generation to generation through oral means. Contemporary advances in digital media and video enable this tradition to be shared with a wider audience.

Our hope is that readers are able to connect with and appreciate these stories in some small way and that we can learn from and be better informed about the uniqueness of each woman's experience without excessive analyses; while also acknowledging that each woman is much more than the few pages that have been allocated to her.

Wahida Shaffi

GLOSSARY

Aalim	A person with sound knowledge of the Holy Qur'an, the Prophetic traditions and Islamic Law
Abba Jee	Father
Ablutions	Ritual washing before prayers
Akharat	Afterlife
Alhamdulilla	Praise be to Allah
Aalima	Female scholar
Allah	The Arabic name for God
Aman	Peace
Appa	Honorific title for older sister
Badmash	Corrupt
Bari	Gifts (usually clothes) given to a daughter for her wedding
Barkat	Blessings
Beta	Child
Bhurka	An outer garment worn by some Muslim women – this could include the covering of the face where only the eyes are visible – also referred to as the niqab
Bindi	An accessory generally worn in the middle of the forehead, common in Hindu cultures
Buddae	Old people
Chaddar	A loose robe worn like a cloak as an outer garment that can cover the head and body
Darood sharif	Salutations to the Prophet Muhammed (pbuh)
Diwalli	Festival of light as celebrated by Hindus
Diya	Lamp for candles usually used for Diwali
Doli	Bridal Palanquin
Dua	Prayer
Dupatta	Headscarf worn loosely around the shoulders or as a head covering, usually to accompany shalwar kameez
Eid	Muslim celebration after Ramadan and Hajj
Eid ul Adha	Festival of sacrifice celebrated by Muslims

Fasting	The ninth Muslim month, Ramadan, is laid down as a month of fasting: an adult must refrain from eating, drinking, smoking, and conjugal relations from dawn to sunset
Fiqh	Science of Islamic law or jurisprudence
Five Pillars	The Five Pillars of Islam, described as the actions which arise out of belief: the declaration of faith (Shahada), Prayer (Salat), Fasting (Sawm), Welfare tax (Zakat), Pilgrimage (Hajj)
Gita	Shortened name of the sacred book of the Hindus
Gora	Colloquial term for white male
Goray	White people
Grahn	Village
Hafiz	A person who has memorised the Quran
Hajj	Pilgrimage to Mecca
Halal	Permitted in Islam (eg, permitted food)
Haram	Prohibited in Islam (eg, food)
Hifz	Memorization of the holy Quran by Muslim's
Hijab	A Muslim woman's head covering – normally it covers all of the hair
Hijabi	A Muslim woman who wears a hijab or head scarf (slang term)
Imam	A person who leads the prayer
Insha'Allah	If Allah wills it/Allah willing
Islam	The faith of Muslims
Islamophobia	Something that goes/is against Muslims
Izzat	Honour
Jayshree Krishna	Hindu greeting
Jihad	In this context refers to the 'internal human Struggle'
Jilbab	Long coat or gown worn by Muslim women
Kalima	This word defines the statement of Declaration of Faith: There is no God and Muhammed is his Prophet
Karbala	City in Iraq particularly holy for Shiites where a holy battle took place
Khuda hafiz	Usually said when departing/God go with you

Madrassa	A place where children learn Quran – supplementary school
Mangal Sutra	This is a symbol of Hindu marriage
Mela	Festival
Mehndi	Henna usually worn on the hands especially for weddings
Mohalla	A neighbourhood or locality in the cities and towns
Muharram Majlisses	A Holy month in Islam when people gather together
Namaste	Hindu greeting
Namaz	Another word for salat or prayer
Nikaah	A formal ceremony meaning a marriage between a man and a woman
Pakoras	A small deep-fried snack with potatoes and other vegetables
Pashto	Language spoken by Pathans
Pathan	A minority ethnic speaking Pashto and living in North Western Pakistan or South Eastern Afghanistan
Purdah	Seclusion, social isolation
Pushto	Language spoken by Pathans
Qaida	An Arabic book for children usually read in the Madrassa
Quran	The sacred book of Muslims
Rakhi	A Hindu custom of tying a band around the wrists of males by females at the festival of Rakasha Bandan
Ramadan	Month of fasting
Rishta	Marriage proposal
Salaam o alaikum	Muslim greeting (Peace be on you)
Salat	Salat or prayer is the second Pillar of Islam – five daily prayer times are laid down: before sunrise, after midday, late afternoon, at sunset and during the night. These are obligatory for all Muslims, unless they are travelling
Salat ul Istikhara	Islamic prayer for guidance
Sari	A female garment in the Indian subcontinent

Shahada	Shahada or the Declaration of Faith: There is no God and Muhammed (pbuh) is his Prophet.
Shalwar kameez	National dress of Pakistan, worn by men and women
Sheikh	A wise person, or an Islamic scholar
Shia	Second largest denomination of Islam
Sirat	Writing detailing the life of the Prophet Muhammed (pbuh)
Sunni	A follower of the largest denomination of Islam
Surah	A chapter of the Quran
Umrah	Lesser Hajj
Walaythee	British
Zabaan	Language/mother tongue

ARSHAD BEGUM AJEEB
THE MAYORESS

If I could give you information of my life it would be to show how a woman of very ordinary ability has been led by God in strange and unaccustomed paths to do in His service what He has done in her. And if I could tell you all, you would see how God has done all, and I nothing. I have worked hard, very hard, that is all; and I have never refused God anything. (Florence Nightingale)

I never thought that this shy little girl from a village would end up being the first ever Asian Lady Mayoress in Great Britain. I never imagined it at all! I was born in Khanyara Sharif. You know there's the town of Mirpur, well Dadyal's the village bit further along from Mirpur and my village is near that. I'm nearly 57 now. I was married at a very young age and I came to England as a young bride when I was just 16. That was 1969. I'd heard really good things about England then. Everybody that went back from England seemed to be well dressed and nicely turned out like gentlemen and everybody was curious to see England for themselves. I wasn't that keen to come here though you know because my entire family, my brothers and sisters, my parents, they were all in my village. It was heart breaking leaving them behind. But my husband was here so I had no choice, I had to come.

You may not believe this but when I first arrived in 1969, for an entire year it felt as though I had been locked up. My husband was working for a housing association then so he'd be out of the door early every morning. We had some family here then but I had to spend the whole day in this big house. I was scared stiff! I felt anxious. And the weather was atrocious – I'd seen nothing like it before – fog, rain and more fog. It was awful. I never went shopping for groceries. I just didn't go out on my own. I preferred to go with my husband who had a better understanding of what was halal, what wasn't. I would cook whatever he brought home. I just thought everything about this country was strange – the streets, the houses, the weather. I was used to sunshine in Pakistan and everything feels open, spacious and bright. I came here in the month of January and it was incredible to me that you didn't see sunshine for days because of all the fog and snow. I missed my parents as well.

Back then we had BBC1 and BBC2 but there was this Asian programme they showed early on Sundays at 7.30am – *Nayee Zindagi Naya Jeevan* or something like that. That was the highlight of our week and we'd set the alarm to wake up in time for that programme on Sundays. You didn't want to risk sleeping through it just because it was in our mother tongue even though it was only 25 minutes long. They'd put on a song at the end as well and we loved that.

There was a Sikh couple in my neighbourhood and they had a little girl, not even a year old. The wife had a machine at home and she did piecework, over locking sweaters. She must have sensed I was only young and how anxious and lonely I was all day, so she said, "Listen Arshad, I have my sewing work to do all day so I can't come and spend the day with you, but you should come over everyday and you can play with my little girl." The arrangement was great for her obviously and I had some company as well and that's how I got through that first year. After a year I had a child of my own and that's when I started to feel a little more settled.

Was it 1977 or '78 when my husband first stood in the elections? I can't remember. He'd always had an interest in politics and he'd go on about it when he got home and I'd think, "Can't we talk about something else?" When he stood for Lord Mayor, I remember him ringing me up to say he'd been elected. I was delighted. It was such a privilege to be elected. That was 22 years ago now. He'd told me what a big deal it would be if he got elected, that he'd be the first Asian Lord Mayor of the country, so I was thrilled that God granted him success. When he was councillor there were times I accompanied him to functions. I didn't enjoy these occasions because I was a homely sort of wife. I preferred to stay home. So I'd seen the Lady Mayoress at these functions and I was impressed by the respect they commanded. People stood up for them so they obviously thought something of them.

I'd told my husband I wouldn't be Lady Mayoress if he got elected. For a start my English wasn't great. I'd been to school in Mirpur and I can read and write Urdu, but it's not like I received a broad education or anything. My dad encouraged me but I refused to go back to school after I got married because I thought the girls would laugh at me because I was married so young. I was painfully shy, still am. I'd spent my whole life at home so I couldn't see how I could carry out such a public role. I had four young children and you know they weren't at an age where they could fend for themselves. My eldest daughter was 15 then and we thought she could stand in for me, but I was worried it would affect her studies since it wasn't a one-off; it would be for a whole year. It wasn't fair on her. In the end, I bit the bullet and agreed.

The decision took me about a week to make and so the preparations began. I was a shy woman who liked my private life but I was going to be a public person with a lot of responsibilities. I went to Pakistan and got myself a new wardrobe. I had to get myself kitted out with some decent clothes – a year's worth of outfits to wear to all these functions I'd have to attend. I had 20 or 22 shalwar kameez stitched. I bought some saris. I needed shoes, handbags, some matching jewellery, accessories. I bought some stuff from Pindi, from Lahore, and Mirpur had good variety as well. That chain you have to wear is really heavy, you know. Your shoulders start to hurt if you keep it on all day. It's solid gold and when the function finished you sent it back. Can you imagine trying to look after that at home! When we went to Pakistan on an official visit, we had a security man with us and he'd take the chain and put it in a safe as soon as the function was over. I told him as well, "This is Pakistan you know. Be careful with that chain here!"

That year we were the second most photographed people in the country – second to Lady Diana. I realised how important it was that my husband was the first ever Lord Mayor of Bradford and I suppose that I was the first Asian Lady Mayoress. Maybe some day we will see the first ever Asian Prime Minister for all people in Britain. I mean now we have people like Shahid Malik, Salma Yaqub, Saeeda Warsi; they represent different parties but the point is Asians are getting involved in such things more and more and more and that is important.

Obviously my husband wasn't just the Lord Mayor for Asians; he was Lord Mayor for everybody. In my role as Lady Mayoress I remember one of my first duties was to open a fair, you know like these mela's for English people, and that was my first TV appearance as well. I was so nervous. I just kept reciting the kalima under my breath to calm my nerves. We had to go to church quite a few times as well and when the English people read from their holy book, I recited my kalima and darood sharif instead. I stood up like they did but I said my own prayers instead. It was a constant struggle to calm my nerves and my husband would say, "Don't worry! They're just people as well like you and me!" He'd remind me, "They invited you! You're here as their guest." It also helped to find people I knew already at these functions. That helped build my confidence. The Chief Exec's wife went everywhere with me, you know when I had to attend something on my own, and that really helped. I don't know if it was a rule they had or if she was doing it especially for me. You get given a prepared speech and you just have to stand up and say it. I could read English a little bit but I practised at home, in front of the kids and they

OUR STORIES, OUR LIVES
ARSHAD BEGUM AJEEB

corrected my mistakes. That was only two or three times that I had to do a speech. Usually it would be the Lord Mayor and my job was to sit beside him, smile and perhaps make small talk with some of the guests. My husband was the one with all the responsibility! He'd be out from early in the morning and he'd be getting back after midnight.

All I'd ever done was look after my house and children, and I learnt a lot because I was put in the deep end and for a very shy person I think I did rather well. But it was a relief when the year ended. I was so grateful that we had served our term with honour and dignity. A year was more than enough though. You see, having a young family made it difficult. Some days we had to attend four or five functions – you'd be going from one to the next and getting back home after midnight. I had young children and I just didn't have time for housework. They provided a woman who could come and stay with the children if we had to attend an evening function. You see, the English are clever in that respect. They know you wouldn't be able to cope with any more than a year.

19

FATIMA AYUB
THE PIONEER

I've seen it around the world, in the poorest countries and in countries riven with conflict…. It is women who are the key to breaking out of poverty, breaking out of stagnation…. It is women who can contribute to achieving real security … not bombs and bullets and repressive governments. (Queen Noor of Jordon)

OUR STORIES, OUR LIVES
FATIMA AYUB

Pioneers always create a space for others to follow and shape other paths and in some ways my mother opened up a path for me and in some ways I'm opening the path up for my daughters. I'm Fatima Ayub. I'm 36 and I have four children. My eldest daughter will be 15 soon – her dream is to become a British female Islamic scholar – there are far too many men and there's a real shortage of good female scholars who can work within the context of Britain. We have a responsibility that is as much ours as anyone else's. And what I mean by that is that we have a responsibility to our community and 'our community' consists of people of all walks of life. My other daughter's 12, mad about football, she's a Gunners' fan, a real Arsenal supporter! Both of them are at boarding school. I've got two younger sons, an eight-year-old and a five-year-old and at the moment I'm expecting my fifth child. My life literally evolves around my children. I'm the second of five children myself, and I'm the eldest daughter. Growing up in Bradford was great, it's a small place and my friends and relatives were all close by, literally streets and doors away. My father was always very supportive and I always saw him supporting my mum. The extended family would think, "Why is he always helping his wife? The daughters are always sat around and the wife is being helped by her husband!" But that's something my dad always did. He always made our breakfast. He helped to put washing out. He even does the cooking now and then. Yesterday he made pakoras for us all. He's always serving us, in a practical sense, he's a really good role model for us all and even for the grandchildren to look up to, and I hope they take something from that because it's important to grow up with secure individuals around you who are not afraid of what people might say.

Most of the people that came here in the early days came from back home to England; to work here, to earn money and culture was something that people held on to. It was something that defined you and gave you a sense of belonging. But at times we have to draw a clear demarcation between culture and religion. I'm not dissing culture in any way because it is extremely important. There's a lot of good stuff in Pakistani and Asian culture that we can take from and celebrate but there's also a lot of negative cultural baggage that passes from parent to child too and we cannot overlook that. I was part of Young Muslims for at least 15 or 20 years, and in 1990, Islamic Society of Britain was formed, and it was for all those people that were in Young Muslims that had grown up, so it was catering for the adults, like the graduate club. I've been

the women's coordinator here in Bradford, and have been in charge of Young Muslims nationally and now I take more of a local role. They were set up to cater for young people's needs – we realised that there were problems young people were facing. They had questions about life in general; identity, etiquettes, gender and all the questions that raises. Young men and women needed people that they could approach about their Islamic identity. People they respected and benefited from and more often than not they were people of a similar age to themselves – so they could connect through language and shared British culture. Most of the workers were volunteers and over the years we have become more and more organised.

In the grand scheme of things we're still a very new community in Britain and sometimes we become impatient. I just have to reluctantly accept the fact that change doesn't come overnight. But it took women like me, back in the day, to take bold steps and change things for our next generation of men and women. What I see nowadays, are more and more women who are strong, they're campaigning; they're working hard and demanding to be heard on every level possible. They're marching for peace and justice, and their own inclusion and participation. They're taking up positions in the community despite the fact that some people may not like that. And they're doing their best to make sure their children are getting more than they had health, education, aspiration wise. We still have a long way to go and sometimes it's really difficult when people are so stuck in their ways! But you know I really do see the Muslim community growing and growing with confidence; whereas the first generation were scared that they may be deported if they challenged authority, the second and third generations are using their democratic rights to challenge and change things and consider themselves British. You still have lots of people who still feel unheard and underrepresented! In fact Iraq was the only time that we saw millions of people of all backgrounds march on the streets of London but no one listened and we ended up going to war for no reason, no evidence at all and they admit it now! Let's not even talk about what's been happening in Gaza – Palestine at the moment. It's incredible that the world sits back while some of the world's most densely populated refugee camps are bombed by the biggest superpower in the Middle East. When I think of all the death and destruction, when I see children dying unnecessarily and parents saying "please help us" it makes my blood boil! As a mother you opt for peace don't you?

Our government also has a lot to answer for when all this legislation treats people unfairly like the anti-terrorism legislation. I've sat with people and consoled them after their homes have been raided. One woman even offered police officers tea! Just shows the extent of hospitality even during hardship. Recently I heard about a Muslim family who were thrown off a plane in America even after they were cleared by the FBI just because other passengers overheard them speaking about the safest place to sit on the aeroplane. You have to ask yourself whether they would have been thrown off if they were non-Muslim? They did this poll on AOL asking a similar question and most people said that they would not have been thrown off if they were non-Muslim. I do question community cohesion and civil liberties at times. I question this idea of equality – 'some are just more equal than others in this world'. I'm sorry but I'm just really passionate about these sorts of issues.

As far as my personal life goes, I've been really blessed; I have been married for 16 years and have been negotiating aspects of my work and family life for years. Nowadays we hear a lot about forced and arranged marriages and I would defy anyone who claims that a forced marriage is acceptable. I can safely say that mine was an arranged marriage through friends and family and we got married on the grounds that we had the same aspirations, the same vision. We both wanted to marry somebody who was practising. So we agreed to marry although he was from outside of the family. In those days getting married outside of the family was a very difficult thing to do. He's a Muslim but at the end of the day my family had their own expectations of where they wanted me to marry. My father and mother alhamdulilla were fine. They were just more worried what the extended family were going to think – you know, "Our daughter's marrying outside the family," so it did take a while to convince them, for them to come round. And alhamdulilla, eventually they did come round. It was all new to them, and they needed time to come round to the idea and I gave them that time, and alhamdulilla eventually they gave their blessings.

My brother knew my husband-to-be and his sister knew me because we were attending the Young Muslims circle. I'd never seen him. And the suggestion came through another couple who said he was looking for a practising girl. I wasn't really interested in marriage but they kept saying, "He's a really good person, why don't you consider him?" So they arranged for me to have a meeting with him while they were present, so there was a third party present. It was a formal meeting where we sat and we spoke. I wasn't really thinking anything. I just thought, 'Well, if he's a good Muslim, and he's of good character, then I would consider him, but I'd only do that once I've met him'. He asked me questions. I asked him questions – you know, what his aspirations were, what his expectations were, if he would allow his wife to work, would she be able to pursue education? I wanted to be active in Young Muslims because that's what I was used to, you know attending circles and camp and organising events for young girls. Would I be able to continue that in married life? Did he have any expectations of me? What kind of expectations were they? So basically he just left it open. He just said, "Whatever you want to do, whatever you're happy with, I'm happy with that."

My hope was that we would grow and learn together and deepen our understanding of Islam – that was my greatest expectation. There's a special prayer called Salat ul Istikhara, it's seeking God's assistance and guidance in any decision you make in your life, so you pray two units of prayer. After those two units, you say a special prayer asking God, "If this situation or this marriage is good for me, then let it happen. And if it's not good for me, then keep it away from me." So I would constantly pray and ask God's guidance on him basically, asking whether he was good for me or bad for me. It's a very pragmatic way of looking at things. So I continued praying that and in my heart I felt content. He'd said yes straight away. He was happy after the first meeting so he was ready to send his parents to my house. I was taking my time on making that decision. It took me a good couple of weeks to make that decision and then he sent his father to my parents' house. My brother had already spoken to my parents that this person's interested and his father's going to come over and ask for Fatima's hand in marriage. The father came and my father didn't give any answer. He didn't say yes or no. It was his first daughter who was getting married. This was somebody from outside the whole extended family, somebody that he didn't know, and he wasn't going to rush into it. He wanted to know that this man was the right person for his daughter so he took his time in meeting and talking to the family, asking other people what this guy is like. He did his research; he did his homework before he gave his blessing.

At the time my extended family weren't very happy with the fact that I'd married outside the family, and it had opened up the gateway for other girls to follow in my footsteps, so it was a very taboo thing. It's just that everybody was marrying inside the family. It's tied to culture and caste which is to do with how your families/ancestors lived in Pakistan and what they did. Although in Islam you can marry anybody as long as he's a Muslim. He can be black, white, yellow; it doesn't matter where he's from – background – caste – as long as he's a Muslim. But when you tell people these sorts of things they find it threatening. The idea that their son or daughter might want to marry a Muslim of different colour or cultural background can be a bit too much, amazing how we complicate things really.

I was just asking for my Islamic rights and that gave me the strength, to be honest with you. In a sense, other girls saw me as a pioneer and afterwards I was a kind of a marriage counsellor for them. People were saying things like, "do a small wedding," just to hide the fact that I was marrying out of the family, and some of them didn't want to know me after the marriage and they didn't want to keep the family links. My mum really changed at that point. She found the voice and courage and I remember her saying, "My daughter didn't come from a rubbish tip! She's our rose and I want to see her happy, no matter what everyone else is saying!" Both of my parents were like rocks for me at that point. Before we got married, we had the engagement process and in that process, we talked to each other on the phone. We were getting to know each other. If I wanted to ask him any questions that I wasn't sure about, any queries I had about him, I'd ring him up and ask him. So it wasn't just one meeting. It was phone conversations and his family would come round; we'd sit and talk. So it was a gradual process. And yes, I was emotionally attached and he was emotionally attached, and yes we did like each other. It wasn't like, "Oh! We got no feelings and it's going to be very cold." You know, there were feelings involved but you control those feelings within the framework of Islam, and in Islam, you don't go out and have courtship in that sense. You don't have a relationship before marriage. I never met him alone until I was married. Never! And that's the beauty about arranged marriages. And they do work!

BARKAT BIBI
DADI MA THE MOTIVATOR

I would like to be remembered as a person who wanted to be free so that other people would also be free and I have learned over the years that when one's mind is made up this diminishes fear; knowing what must be done does away with fear. (Rosa Parks)

I don't know what year I was born because in those days we didn't have ways of documenting people's dates of birth. But I must be in my 80s now according to the date on my passport – probably even more! And I guess because I've lived in this country for such a long time I have become walaythee (British) myself! I live on my own in a big old house near Lister Park and Oak Lane, it has central heating so it's nice and warm and I've got a stair lift that I hardly ever use because it scares me.

I was born in Pakistan. We were only small when our father passed away. I've never even seen a picture of him. I don't know what he looked like. It's not like we had cameras or anything in the villages then. There was nothing in the grahn (village) – no cameras, no TV, no microwaves, no cassette players, nothing at all. We grew up at a time of war and food like flour and sugar were rationed, entire families had to share; sometimes you had to go without and sleep on empty stomachs. You had to patiently endure the hardships. Pakistan was our beloved country, a source of our pride and our joy: a young country trying to find its feet and a lot of blood and sweat was shed to create it. In those days life was so different from the life I have now and the life my children and grandchildren have.

People trusted the decisions that their parents made for them. My elders used to tell me that when I was born my grandma tied a piece of string to my wrist, and she told my father, "Son, I've promised your daughter to your brother's son." Can you imagine! A piece of string! A piece of black string! That was my fate – so I'd been promised! My father agreed to the marriage. In those days people really trusted one another, there was loyalty, wisdom and love at the heart of the decisions that our elders made. We didn't have much money, food or belongings but we had love and respect! It was your parents that made these decisions for you; that's how it was done! We used to have a saying that, 'Even if you're parents arranged your marriage with a donkey, you wouldn't refuse.' It was a society based on conformity. I know it sounds quite funny but there is a lot of wisdom in that expression though times have changed considerably now – society is far more nonconformist and it's all about the individual and what their needs are. My older brother looked after me a lot – the one who used to own Sufi Textiles on White Abbey Road. I'd already been promised to my cousin and my brother sorted out the arrangements. I was only eleven and a half then. That wasn't particularly young for a girl to be getting married in them times. I was skinny as a rake I was.

You'd have been shocked! I looked like a doll! On the same night my husband was called to the army and I stayed at his sister's house. I still remember it clearly. Of course I knew what was happening on the day of my wedding. I was in a (doli) bridal palanquin being carried around the neighbourhood. My older brother symbolically gave his shoulder to the palanquin as well, and I remember he cried and cried that he was giving away his baby sister. There was no dowry for me. I had nobody to give me one! Jewellery, yes I suppose! I got silver ankle bracelets, silver bangles and silver earrings. We couldn't think about gold, no one had gold in them days. I carried on living with my brother for a short while then moved with my husband's sister. A few years later my husband returned, I was much older then.

My husband's sister was married and already settled in England. They all helped out financially and eventually she called for her brother, me and our children and that's how we came. The government in England encouraged people to come to help in the factories because they needed workers. They needed us and we needed them. It is still their country. Oh, we were in the tiniest aeroplane and my children were very small. And they were so scared that they threw up all the way to London. And that's when I first saw Goray (white) people at Heathrow Airport. I couldn't believe my eyes that these people had such fair skin! Back then I thought they were such beautiful people, so young and white skinned. I remember thinking that God's creation was amazing! Over the years I've got used to looking away when they kiss each other or when they're legs are bare. You just have to try not to look. You're supposed to cover it all up aren't you, that's what the Quran says. It doesn't feel right, does it? But what do you do when everyone's at it now!

Once we had settled we got a house of our own; the extended family, were so important in the early days. My husband used to work in a factory where they make parts for aeroplanes, welding parts together or something. They'd be suspicious if there was a beard doing that sort of work now ... with everything that's happening. He used to come home really tired and his beard would be all joined up and greasy with bits that had melted away with the heat. Every week without fail right up until he retired he would hand over his earnings to me. A lot of us women used to save money by joining a committee (community saving scheme), it's usually managed by a group of women and you put money to one side every week and by the end of the year or however long you get what you have saved. It's a brilliant way of saving especially if you have responsibilities back home and here. My beloved husband – who I never referred to by his name because it is a sign of disrespect – would take £5 for his cigarettes and other bits and bobs but would give the rest to me to spend accordingly on household bills, food, children's clothing. We shared a good life together. I used to walk to the town centre and get the groceries; there weren't as many shops as you see nowadays. I remember that everything tasted so different and the shape of the vegetables was strange compared to vegetables back home. Here you have round tomatoes and in Pakistan they're longish. I missed the food, the water, the taste of salt lassi that we used to have with roti and green chillie chutney, umm, that was really something, simple food but tasty. Nowadays the kids buy takeaways and eat gand blah (rubbish) when there is much more barkat (blessing) in home cooked food.

I was responsible for the home. My husband was responsible for work. It was a partnership. People give up on marriage so quickly nowadays. A woman is the foundation of the family or the house. She is the strength, the glue that cements everything together that then helps to build a solid structure, and then after that each part of the house needs others. But if the foundation is weak then the house falls or if each part doesn't play its role then the structure will begin to erode.

I made sure I did my best for my children when it came to education. Even though I can't read or write I encouraged my children. My second son Arshad was the first one to get a degree and my youngest Sajid went to Cambridge University. No one else in my relatives has been to Cambridge. It's the mother that educates her children, and I've done the best with my children. Now it's up to them how they live their lives. I want my next generation to make something of themselves in this country. It's a lot fairer for the girls and boys nowadays not like the olden days. I couldn't even read the Quran until I was about 40, and I can just about sign my name in English now. It would have been good if I'd been to school. I might not have struggled so much. I could have done things for myself – speaking English, maybe writing a letter. But I can't blame anyone, can I! Who was going to educate me? I was just a child when my father died. The war meant lots of people became displaced and there was no time for school. It was survival for lots of people. I didn't even

know what education was. We didn't even have a school in our village. Hindus and Sikhs owned schools and the nearest was in Mirpur. Village folk never bothered with educating their daughters then. They used to say, "Why bother with our daughters? What are they going to do with it besides writing love letters to boys and becoming corrupt? Daughters are better off illiterate!" But you know these people were so uncivilised and illiterate, they didn't even know what education was. People were simple then, weren't they! People lived off the land, worked hard, and tried to fill their stomach and bide their time; that was it! Without education a person has no value. I was the first woman to send my daughter to school in the village. They would say, "Don't send your daughter she will become badmash (corrupt)." I said to them, "If she really wanted to do anything wrong she would find other ways." Nowadays it's the boys that are sitting on their backsides and doing nothing whereas the girls are doing well in every area. I think I have always been headstrong and I speak my mind. If I don't like something I will say it – that's me – I don't like all of this behind people's back stuff! When you have to speak you speak – no messing around!

The world has changed a lot since I was young. I don't think society appreciates just how much of a struggle us buddae (old people) went through. My worry is that children of the next generation will forget their zabaan (language) and their culture; you know where they came from. Things have also changed a lot for women, girls can drive, go to university, they are living a luxury life. Back in my days we had to give birth on stones, worked in the fields in the heat and these days you have hospitals to take care of your every need and cosy jobs in offices. They travel all over too, in the old days girls would not have been allowed to travel by themselves at all. I'm not bitter; we have a lot to be thankful for and I'm pleased to see such change. Ahhh, you know ... I do think sometimes that I would have achieved so much if I was young now because there are so many more opportunities. The technology has changed so much as well – you can send things and they get to different places in seconds. My granddaughters are always on their phones and computers listening to music you know, prah, prah, prah ... it does your head in!

Despite all of these changes, WE CANNOT afford to forget the stories of our older generation. My only dua (prayer) is that my children won't forget to tell their children what the first generation actually went through to help create a better life for young people now!

NASREEN CHOUDHURY

FROM SYLHET TO ILKLEY

The education and empowerment of women throughout the world cannot fail to result in a more caring, tolerant, just and peaceful life for all.
(Aung San Suu Kyi)

There are lots of Sylheti people who live in England. From my family it was only me that moved here. I got married to a man from England, Bangladeshi of course. I was 18, so I was quite excited. It was England, you know! When we were small we used to think that there were apple trees and grape trees in the streets and that the pavements were made of gold. And I thought it would be like the pictures in the television and books. You have this beautiful image in your mind of how things will be like. The reality is hard work!

At that time my husband was working in a carpet mill as a supervisor. He has a big family so he had to maintain them as well in Bangladesh, sending money from here. He had six brothers and three sisters; my father-in-law was only a headmaster in Bangladesh so life was quite hard for him. When I first came to England I remember that there was a house in Queens Road and I stayed with some family friends for a year. Straight away I had a little baby and then I started struggling because I was young. I couldn't speak English. Now people who want to come to England have to do a citizenship and English exam – I have heard it's really hard. Even people that have lived here all their lives don't understand half the questions. When I came we had nothing like that. I just knew 'yes', 'no', things like that. Gradually I thought, 'If I'm going to stay here, I have to learn!' I wanted to say something but I couldn't say it. I'd be thinking, 'Oh, it's going to be wrong.' Then I realised it will probably keep me down, so I kept getting things wrong until eventually I started to get them right. I was just trying, through watching television with the children, going to the shops and by watching people you know how they were talking and how they were interacting.

In 1973, my husband opened a restaurant in Ilkley. He had an accident in the factory you see and lost his hand and he couldn't do any other job. So you know like every Asian, he started a restaurant business. They say that the main dish in England is curry now! Curry Capital! There were loads of restaurants in Bradford but there was no Indian restaurant in Ilkley. At that time, if a Bangladeshi person came here as an engineer or doctor, they couldn't get into the education system if they hadn't studied here and now they are desperate and there are lots of foreign doctors, nurses, teachers from all over the world coming to work here. We moved to Ilkley as well. Ilkley is a tourist town so people come from all over the world, and we were recommended in all the restaurant books and things so the restaurant was getting famous, famous and famous. We had a good lifestyle. We bought a house straight away but it was close enough to Bradford. I couldn't live in Ilkley without Bradford because my people are there and I do all my shopping there. Ilkley is a very small but wealthy place. One of the wealthiest in the UK I think. It was a nice beautiful time. People were very nice and friendly. In Bradford you can get abused but I don't think in Ilkley, luckily I never ever felt racially threatened or anything. I always wore my sari even now I wear my sari. My husband used to say, "Whatever dress you wear, they won't call you English so what's the point wearing English dresses?" I mean, they don't call you English if you wear trousers, jeans, tights, whatever it is. So I thought why don't I just stick to my own sari instead? I don't think it's very convenient dress especially in this country because in windy weather it gets blown. But when I go out in a sari, the old ladies say, "You look nice with this beautiful sari. Don't get Westernised!" I don't know if they're joking or seriously saying it, but I think they are being serious. It makes me feel proud! Ilkley is a lot quieter compared to Bradford and there are less Asian people. There were only two Bangladeshi families or something back then.

Everything was going so well, we had a home, business, children were good but then my husband passed away in 1984. He had a heart attack and died suddenly. He was 54 and I was 10 or 12 years younger than him. So I was left with the children and the struggle began!

I didn't have time to sit down and think, 'Oh he's gone. Why has he gone?' I couldn't afford to get into depression and all this. Because I had children and one of them was about to do his O'levels, and my children were still in private school. So I thought, 'If I'm going to breakdown what's going to happen to them!' So then I had to run the business all by myself – straight from housewife to businesswoman! I couldn't close the restaurant. There was something in my mind that just said 'you just have to do it', so I did. Living with my husband, I observed how he maintained the business. We already had the staff, I knew who the delivery man was, who the supplier was, who the accountant was, and everyone helped me a lot you see. They were very good. I had to make sure the business was running well. I mean there were lots of deliveries coming and I had to do the shopping in Bradford. Then there was the management side, paying the staff at the end of the week, and all that. It was quite hard duty – that's why all my hair has gone grey, you see.

At the time lots of people, you know my friends and everybody were saying that I should get married again, "One day when the children go away, you will be on your own." But I thought that if I was to bring somebody new into the family and if he did not get on well with my two sons, then what would I do! Then I'll be in big trouble you know. I can't choose! I can't say that I'm going to leave my sons! So that's when I made the decision that I'm not going to get married. After all, my husband had given his life to me so I decided – no marriage. I mean, if he had gone with somebody else, probably I would re-marry straight away. I'd show him, "If you go with somebody else, I can do this as well!" But he gave his life to me so I was committed to him and will be until the end. It was my choice and I don't regret it. I put my children on the right track. We were lucky enough to send our three children to private school. They had done their O'levels, A'levels and they had gone to university. So I finished the business after four and a half years. It was too much pressure you know. I wasn't getting any younger and there were staff problems you see, because lots of people live in Bradford and they don't want to travel to Ilkley. And these days people pick up staff with their big car but I couldn't do this because I'm a woman. Lots of things. So I thought, 'While the business is nice, just sell it.'

You know my husband, just like all Asian people, he wanted his children to be doctors. I don't know! They think that a doctor is something BIG! But now everybody is suffering. It's so difficult to get into a job because there are so many doctors now. My son wanted to be a doctor, and he's a doctor now – his own choice. My husband wanted my daughter to be a doctor but she said, "No, I want to be an economist," so he said it's ok. You can't pressure children. My main ambition was to give them the best education because I realise that the world is getting so competitive, and if they don't get a good education, they're going to suffer. So I said to my husband, who was my rock, "If I need to work, I'll work for the school fees," but luckily our business was doing so well, so we didn't have any difficulty. I didn't study very far in Bangladesh. I passed my matriculation and I had done my intermediate. I could speak a little bit of Urdu because Urdu was compulsory when Bangladesh was East Pakistan. But five or six years ago, when my children were grown, I did Welfare & Society

O'level. It was just a hobby. And then I have done a one-year Arabic course. Then I have done Study Able, and then they said, "You can go into teaching!" and I said, "No more studying. That's it!" I'm glad I have retired. I have worked hard; people work too hard in Britain and the government is always telling you to work, work, work until you die. In the rest of Europe it is different.

When I was younger I wanted to be a lawyer but my mother got me married. I had no choice. Still they do this, when they find a good husband they want the girl to get married. I think that you can have both marriage and education but it's easier when you are single. I didn't let that happen to my daughter. She is educated. She has done her graduation. Now she has finished her MBA from Chicago University. I helped her a lot. I went there to look after her little baby till she finished her MBA. I think it is a big asset, isn't it – educating children. Nobody can take that away. I mean, you can leave them thousands and thousands of pounds, but if you don't educate your children, it will all be lost. That's what my mother said to us even though she wasn't educated. "Nobody can take your degree away from you," so that's what was in my mind.

When your children are educated you have to make sure that you also select a compatible partner for them not just give them to anyone. I got my daughter married. I introduced one boy to her. I said, "There's a boy, he's educated, he's from this family. Talk with him. If you are interested then we'll talk." And they were talking to each other, sometimes emailing each other, and after a few talks, she said, "It's ok. You can go ahead." Nowadays it is very hard for parents to find compatible partners for their children. Gone are the days where you used to take them back home. Now you have these match making things going on, you have to be careful you know. I'm trying to get my son married. If he chooses anybody, they should be Muslim. It would be better, isn't it, to get married to a Muslim person, but I don't mind a convert and whatever career path she is on, it's ok. It's nothing specific I want. You know, just normal – a nice family girl, who comes from a nice family, educated, well behaved, that's it. My son will be 30 and she will be 26 or 27. I don't want a father–daughter age gap like we used to. Preferably Bangladeshi but I don't mind different because they are living in a country where they all speak English so they can communicate with each other. If my son finds somebody himself and providing that she's Muslim – then good. If she's not Muslim, then you know I have to ask him what's going on. Then I will have to say, "If you're not marrying a Muslim, then I will not be with you! It's an important thing, religion!"

Identity is a good thing. I go to Bangladesh to see my brothers and sisters. We live in Sylhet. It's the northern part of Bangladesh and it's almost next to the Indian border. Sylhet has lots and lots of tea gardens and the natural beauty is quite nice, a bit like Ilkley Moors. I cry every time I leave Bangladesh, still! I don't feel like I'm a second class citizen there. I feel that it's MY country. Over here, sometimes I still feel we are second class citizens! You know you are different! I mean, I know I am British but I am Bangladeshi British. Bangladesh is my country. Probably my son, he is born in this country, so probably he will think this is his country. I am not born in this country and that's probably why I think I don't belong to this country, even though I spent most of my life here. But when I go to Bangladesh, they call us Londoni. They say Londoni because we don't belong to Bangladesh anymore – we have got British passport. They say, "You don't understand our culture and things because you live in England now." That's why sometimes I say, "We don't belong to anywhere. We don't belong to England and we don't belong to Bangladesh." That makes me feel like I'm just floating somewhere in between!

I am becoming more religious. Probably when I was 16, I didn't know anything about religion. I only knew that you have to do namaz five times and even that we didn't do. Now I think about akharat when I have to go in front of God. You see God says, "I have sent you there for the time being. You are only there temporarily. Do whatever you want to do the right way. Then you have to come back to me and answer to me." I do believe in this. Now I think at least I have got time, at least I can do some good thing. In the past mosques just taught Arabic and no translation – how can you learn? I can read all the Islamic books and I can watch Islamic programmes and I can read the Quran with translation. This is the thing that makes me read more Quran everyday, and I think, 'If I go to the cinema, I will miss one namaz.' Probably if I didn't believe that I wasn't going back to God, I would be going to the cinema and watching more TV. Probably I will be different.

Islam is always in the media nowadays, always Muslims are doing this and Muslims are doing that! These last few years, terrorism has not helped us Muslims at all. In Islam, suicide bombings are forbidden in the Quran; how can Muslims do these things? I don't think they are Muslim at all, you know killing innocent people. This is not jihad at all! I remember it clearly, on September 11th 2001 my sister who had come from Bangladesh was watching TV and I was in the kitchen. And she was saying to me, "Look Appa, there's a plane gone into the building!" She wasn't hearing or understanding the news because she doesn't understand English. I thought that she was probably watching a movie. Then she said, "Oh, another plane has gone into another building." So I thought, 'What is she talking about?' and I came and saw the breaking news. My daughter was working in London at the time. She rang me and said that all of them were asked to go home and the office she was working in would be closing up because there was one plane missing in America and they thought that one was probably coming to London. I was worried for my daughter and told her to look after herself. It was shocking!

After all of the things that have gone on in the world, there is no free speech for Muslims in America – you know that! Like lecturing and things, they have a complete watch on you and what you are saying. Lots of clerics have visa problems when they go to America. It's worrying you know, it's Muslim, Muslim, Muslim. With Thatcher it was always miners, miners, miners. Why are the West interfering with the Middle East? Why do you want democracy in the Middle East? There's no democracy in Saudi Arab, there's no democracy in Kuwait; everybody is king and queen or a dictator. But they are living in peace aren't they? They're after Iran now too! So all of a sudden the West decides they want to put democracy in different parts of the world. If you want oil, pay them and they will give you oil. Do the business but stop interfering in people's lives! Their interference bothers me! I just want them to leave them alone!

ELANA DAVIS
MUSIC 'N' MOTHERHOOD

I don't think of myself as a poor deprived ghetto girl who made good. I think of myself as somebody who from an early age knew I was responsible for myself, and I had to make good. (Oprah Winfrey)

You only realise how precious motherhood is when you actually become a mother you know! My mum was the only one from her family to be born in England, everyone else was born in Jamaica. I have a brother and sister from my step dad. He's really cool. He's always treated me like his own. Whatever them lot get, I get, and if ever I need anything he's there. My mum got diagnosed with epilepsy when she had my younger sister and then a couple of years ago she got diagnosed with paranoid schizophrenia. In these sorts of situations the family just pull together – it's hard but you learn to manage. I did a lot of things like getting my brother and sister ready and taking them to school. I used to get away with everything at school because they knew I was late because I'd be dropping them lot off. I even got out of an exam early once just because I said I was going to pick them up, and I wasn't! I used to go to church when I was little, like seven or eight. But me and my cousin used to hide or pretend we were sleeping so they didn't take us to Sunday School because we never liked it. My uncle took us to church on Gaythorne Road – the Light of the World or something like that. I don't know why we went because no one was religious. They were Rastafarian but they weren't religious.

Leeds Road was our patch. We used to hang around Seymour Park. All my friends were Asian. There were me and a white girl and all the rest were Asian boys. There was no black people, no coloured people. There was a few black girls but they moved out. I didn't like hanging round with girls anyway because they were too bitchy, so I was mates with all these Asian lads. We never looked at the colour of their skin or anything like that. Obviously we knew that our friends went to mosque and stuff like that. That was just normal to us. The thing is, we could knock on any of them boys' door and their parents didn't think, 'Oh! There's a girl knocking at the door!' Everyone knew we were all friends and we all hung around together. So it wasn't like hiding on the streets – we just sat on the streets and we all walked to school together. I used to write music at school and I loved dance – street dancing – and I used to get out of lessons to go and teach dance to other classes. So I always wanted to do something with dancing or music. In my GCSEs I got the highest grade in music.

I've known my husband since I was 15. I was really good friends with his brother because he was in my class at school. But when we started at upper school, we had this new group and we all used to walk to school together and you know chill out on the streets. I didn't think he would still be here – no, did I heck! He was my best friend at first and I used to tell him everything. Any secrets I did have I used to tell him anyway so we got close like that. He was my first proper boyfriend. When I was in the sixth form at school, a social worker helped me to get a flat because of special circumstances – I got pregnant when I was 16. I'm in my early 20s now. I found out after I went for a test at the Information shop. I was really scared what people would think because it was at a time when there was all this talk about high teen pregnancies. When you're that age you make mistakes – we're human! But you learn with experience, sometimes we make BIG mistakes and learn the hard way and I guess that's what happened in my case! His family didn't know anything about the child until after he was born because it's all about not hurting people. A lot of these boys, they're too scared of their mum and that's what it was.

When I converted, some people thought I did it for show. I've got to the point where I'm not stressing myself over it. Leave them to it! I'd been reading books on Islam when I was pregnant because I knew that my boyfriend wanted to bring Raheem up as a Muslim. I picked the name. I called my son Raheem. I didn't want a popular name and I didn't want a name that reminded me of someone I went to school with, and I liked the meaning because it means merciful. I made that decision that if my son's going to be Muslim, there's no point me doing whatever because that's just being a hypocrite and showing him two different sides, which I don't think is right. So I started reading up. There's a Muslim guy on my mum's street who always brings me books to have a look at, like basic stuff like what is Islam, the five pillars and stuff. I got all these name books and learnt all this stuff about what you have to do when you're having a baby, like shaving the head and circumcising boys. I never even asked questions about it really – I just did it and got everything sorted myself. Obviously I know loads of Pakistanis and I'm welcome into a lot of these people's homes so obviously I see this stuff happening, so it just came normal to me. My sister used to wear Pakistani clothes just to be like everybody else. My brother and sister used to go to mosque on a regular basis because their friends were Muslim and they went. My brother only stopped going when he was nine or 10 because someone told him he needed circumcising. I don't think he knew what it was but obviously one of the kids must have told him they'd have to chop his willy off or something like that, so he never went back!

Because I've grown up round here, I know everybody. And this woman was asking me if my son's a Muslim – he was only about three months then – and I think by then I'd just started calling myself a Muslim. I'd read these books but this Shahada, like the actual converting, that wasn't something I knew about or anybody had told me about. It was just that I called myself a Muslim. I covered my head as well odd times but I think I did it because I was cold though! So this woman asked me to come to this mosque down at Garnett Street and she said they do women's circles with talks in English for women like me. So after a couple of weeks of going, this woman goes, "Are you a Muslim?" So I said, "Yeah!" So she went, "Have you took your Shahada?" And I said, "What?" So she said, "Have you said: 'there is only one God and Muhammed is his Messenger'?" So I was like, "No!" So she explained that this is what you have to say to be a Muslim. Now, I knew what that prayer was because I used to say it to my son all the time. So the woman asked me if I wanted to do it and I was right enthusiastic and I were right happy so I went, "Yeah!" So I got up in front of these hundreds of women, yeah, and on the microphone I said these words. My blood was rushing and I were just really happy.

The main thing that appealed to me was bringing my son up Muslim. You see for me, my family don't eat pork because Rastafarians don't eat pork and they don't drink either. My mum's only ever cooked halal food anyway. She never went to the butchers because they have pork there and she doesn't eat it. I was a tomboy anyway so I never wore skirts and I was always covered up, so I haven't changed anything really at all. We had actually tried to get married when I was pregnant with my first son and a lot of the mosques wouldn't do it because we were so young. A lot of parents, if they find out their child has gone and done the Nikkah, which is the Islamic marriage, the parents go to these people in the mosque and cause them a lot of trouble. So a lot of the Imams at the mosque said no. But when Raheem was about four months old, I basically decided that there's no point me practising and learning about Islam if I'm going to sleep with my partner outside marriage. So we did the Nikkah in the back of a bookshop in Manningham Lane and then we came home and watched *Eastenders*. And I've carried on living in my house as a single parent and he's carried on living with his mum and family.

I'm happy with my life: I have three beautiful boys. He comes every day. We're together every day. He goes to work. I go wherever I please with my three kids and I don't have to be home for a certain time. I'm my own person. So I have a marriage but I don't have all the stresses of it! I hope he'll get a backbone and stand up to his mum though – I'm not going to wait here all my life. I think for a single parent with three children I do really well! I have to be responsible – no choice, I'm streetwise. I'm smart and I have hopes for my future. I do loads for my community juggling work commitments with motherhood. I don't care what colour or religion people are – I love giving. I don't just wanna be a 'stay-at-home mum'. I know that if I bring my boys up right, they're my community's future. I want them to grow up responsible you know hard working men, not ones that end up on drugs and messing their lives up. I see and hear about dealers and all that stuff all the time in the news and in the community. I want my boys to grow up as men you know responsible! Not mummy's boys! The women in the community are doing amazing things. They really are getting out there showing what they're made of. But the boys they're just getting left behind. I want my boys to be educated, go to uni, travel give something back, not be the types of men who take and take and take and just don't know how to respect women or themselves. So I'm strict but fair with my boys!

I've learnt all my kids how to pray and I've taught them their surahs. Till this day I read half of it in Arabic and half of it in English. God knows I'm trying my best. I've sent them to mosque, not their dad. I've sent them to mosque because I can't learn them everything. It's like I don't know how to read Arabic myself so they need to go to mosque.

I've always worn the headscarf on and off. People should have the choice if they want to wear it, we can't be like the French and other places where they've banned it. I used to wear it most of the time in winter, but sometimes, like my mum lives at the end of the street, so sometimes I won't wear it if I'm just going there. It's when I go out and about where I will wear it. Odd days I don't wear it. Sometimes I need a bit of air and I get really bad spots under my chin, you know when it gets too warm. And when I've done my hair! Because sometimes I like to do my own hair with extensions and stuff, so if I do that, I'm not wasting my time for it to sit under my scarf! People need to see it. But that's not very often. Normally I just put my hair in a bobble and put my scarf on. A lot of women just throw the scarf on their head anyway, not like wearing the full hijab.

But even though I'm a Muslim I still listen to music and I love music. Some scholars say it's haram and some scholars say it's not, but it's different people's perceptions and they can't agree to it. I don't go out clubbing and I listen to music and dance in my own house, and it's not something that I think I'm doing wrong. I'm into my Chris Brown's, Neo's Destiny Child and all that. No one really tells me what is wrong with listening to music. You get odd little kids saying it – "that's haram that is." But I teach dance at Carlton Bolling School. We do street dance. We do a bit of Bollywood as well. With street dancing you do a lot of body popping and flipping and jumping around and stuff. You have to stick to your moves. It's like hip hop music basically. I like a bit of garage music and baseline, and I like Janet Jackson's dancing, but we don't do a lot of shaking bums and shimmying and stuff. It depends what the girls feel comfortable in doing. Someone told me actually that I shouldn't wear my scarf because I taught dance. I think if you listen to what everybody's got to say, you will get confused, and at the end of the day, I became a Muslim for myself. I'll learn myself, and if I do something wrong, that is something that I'm going to have to deal with, with God – nobody else. And I'll just try my best to do my best.

I do like being a Muslim. I think I'm doing it because I want to, and to show my faith to everybody, and to myself. I read namaz because I want to read it. And obviously I've got loads of wishes that I want to get fulfilled so I say my prayers.

NATASHA ALMAS FELL
IDENTITY

Far away, there in the sunshine are my highest aspirations. I may not reach them, but I can look up and see their beauty, believe in them, and try to follow where they lead. (Louisa May Alcott)

My name's Natasha and I'm 14 years old and when I grow up I either want to be an extreme sports instructor, a marine biologist or a Charlie's Angel! People at school say I'm not a Muslim. I don't go to mosque and wear a headscarf and I'm not really that religious, so they think I call myself it just because my mum's Muslim. My dad's not because he's white. I consider myself Muslim because I've been brought up that way. I believe in the same things, so I eat halal meat – it's been killed in a different way. My English friends eat pig and non-halal food and I don't. My mum's taught me to check for the vegetarian sign on the front of foods and if it's chicken or something, then to check it's halal, and to check for gelatine. My mum says I should eat halal food, but that she's not going to make me do anything that I'm not happy with, like go to mosque every evening or anything.

When I was about seven, my next door neighbour was Pakistani. She's moved away now. She was a year older than me and she used to go to mosque and she'd wear shalwar kameezes and I didn't. I guess it did make me think like, 'Why don't I do them things?', but then I've just been brought up not really religious and we do things that are in my Pakistani culture but are also in English culture as well. When people see you and ask what race you are, they usually say, "Well, you're obviously English because you're not really dark skinned." So you just say, "Pakistani" and they're like, "Oh, she's half!" But if I had to ever write it down for a form or something, my mum would just say, "Write British Pakistani." They were just showing me what they both are. My mum would say Pakistani because she wanted me to realise that I'm not just one culture I think. And then my dad would say English. I don't mind being half and half because it makes you different. I don't mind being different. If you forgot about my skin colour, you'd probably think I was English – it's only if you see my mum that you'd know otherwise....

I can't speak Urdu fluently like I can English but I know phrases and stuff like 'hello', 'goodbye' and 'how are you', just little things like that. I wish I knew more because when we go away to Pakistan, everyone's talking and I don't understand it. When you were in the street or something in Pakistan, people just looked at you like, "You're coming to Pakistan and you don't know Urdu!" My relatives over there speak English and Urdu but the main conversation would be in Urdu. It's just handy to know another language. And when we're all at my grandma's house in Bradford as well, I don't understand what they're saying. You want to be more of a part of it. It's better to be in the conversation. It doesn't upset me or anything; I just go and watch TV or something instead, but if they're talking about plans for the weekend or something, then my mum's got to explain it to me after, and it would just be easier for everyone if I could understand.

Most of my boundaries are not to do with being a Muslim; they're to do with what my parents would like, no matter what my religion is. I'm obviously not allowed to drink or take drugs but even if I was, I probably wouldn't anyway because I just don't want to get into that. I'm allowed to go to parties, like my friends' birthdays, but I do have a curfew but if I have to be back in for let's say nine, it's not because I'm a Muslim and I'm not allowed to stay out. It's because my parents want me to be safe.

I think I first fasted when I was seven, because everyone at school was doing it and everyone at home was doing it, and I wanted to give it a go. I wanted to know what it would feel like. You don't feel left out if you don't fast, but you do feel more a part of everything if you do it. You do get really hungry but I guess you've just got to do things that keep your mind off it. At lunchtime at primary school there was about 30 Asian people at our old school, and they had this room for people that fasted so they didn't have to be around the kids that were having their lunch. And everyone was so surprised to see me there because they always thought I was English and not a Muslim. They were all saying, "Are you Muslim? Are you Muslim? I thought you were English! Aren't you fully white?" After that, they were friendlier. They'd be like, "Do you want to play with us?" My grandma's really religious. She does the namaz five times a day and she reads the Quran. She said "well done" and I think she was proud.

We celebrate Eid and Christmas. People at school celebrate one or the other but I celebrate both because I'm English and Pakistani so we celebrate both the cultures. On Eid we get new clothes and we go round to my grandma's and we eat lots of food and we get Eid money – that's money that you get on Eid from people that are older. You give it to people that are younger than you. I think the going rate's like £10 or £20 from one person. My mum's family celebrate Christmas as well although it's not really part of their culture, but I guess because we're in England,

and mostly everyone in England celebrates Christmas, so I guess it's like an extra celebration you can do. We cook a halal turkey and everything. I think I prefer Christmas though just because it's bigger.

SENSEI MUMTAZ KHAN
No Mercy!

*I am only one; but still I am one. I cannot do everything, but still I can do
something; I will not refuse to do something I can do.*
(Helen Keller)

My name is Mumtaz, I'm 35 years old. I was born in Little Horton, the Bradford 5 area. I'm a ju–jitsu teacher so most of my students call me Sensei, which is the Japanese word for a teacher of martial arts. I founded Onna Ju-Jitsu club. I chose the name because I wanted something that would represent me and the word Onna translates as 'woman' in Japanese. It started off with just me and two loyal students, Ian Margerison and Shannon Gibbon. And now I lead a group of instructors, delivering to over 800 people a week and almost 50% that learn are female and the numbers are growing. Maybe some of them will participate in the Olympics in 2012!

My parents came from Peshawar, so they're Pathan, and I think it was the late '50s. My dad came over first, and he was working and established himself and then my mum came over. I'm the youngest of seven. The three eldest were born in Pakistan, and the other two brothers, one sister and myself were born here. My mum was born in Pakistan obviously and she was orphaned at a very young age, maybe three, and was brought up by aunts and uncles. It's a completely different culture to where we are and a different time as well. You've got to remember she was born in 1929 so when she married my dad, she was about 12 and he was about 16. They were first cousins as well so they both shared the same grandfather, which is not uncommon within the culture. She'd had children very young as well. I think she'd had four that were stillbirths. My mum couldn't read or write anything. She could speak some English but very basic. No education whatsoever! But it was never an issue that she couldn't read. It didn't matter.

Growing up skin colour wise, because I was fairer than some of the other children that I used to go to school with, they always assumed that I was of dual heritage – what they called half caste. I can't speak Urdu. I speak Pushto as a dialect which is what Pathans speak so I was always a slight outcast within the Pakistani community, so all my friends when I was young were either, English, Afro Caribbean or different nationalities. The Pakistani girls would be watching Indian films and I didn't because I didn't speak the lingo so you just felt a bit left out. It's very subtle. You'd be at school and people would be talking in Urdu and you'd be thinking, 'I haven't got a clue what they're saying.' Even though at some level they probably didn't mean to, but you felt excluded. I just felt I couldn't communicate with them.

As a child we were sent to mosque to learn to read the Qaida, which is kind of like the A B C in Arabic and Urdu, and then you go on to reading the Quran. My mum unfortunately couldn't read so she'd send me off to mosque, and of course the mosque in those days, the environment was very very strict. If you didn't know what you were doing, the teacher would crack you across the head with a stick, and that was common practice, so people would be getting hit all the time. Now all mosques have to follow child protection procedures. I didn't have a cat in hell's chance of learning to read because the lady who was teaching us was speaking Urdu and she was teaching us to read Arabic. It's like a Chinese-speaking person trying to teach Russian; you've got to know one of the languages to learn the other! So I used to just go with my Qaida, which was my book, put it to one side, go and play with my friends outside in the street, and keep an eye out when the kids were finishing mosque, and then just go home and say, "Yeah, I've been." And I did that for months! It wasn't working so my mum just gave up on it.

I was very very quiet as a person, probably low self-esteem. All I did was try and fit in. I used to do Ramadan which is fasting and I did that from the age of 11 or 12 years old. I never kind of did it from a religious point but I think it was the only time I felt part of the community because everybody was fasting. So you had something in common with every other Muslim person that was there and everybody else at school so you knew you were all in it together – hungry and thinking, 'We need something to eat and drink,' and then you'd go home, and obviously if your family's fasting as well, you feel part of it. I always had a choice – it wasn't a case of 'We're not feeding you for a month and you have to fast.' In all fairness, I actually used to enjoy fasting because it was a time when I actually felt part of a community. In that respect, I think Ramadan is quite special.

School can be a rather daunting place. At school, you make that decision whether you actually want to engage yourself in terms of cigarettes, drugs, alcohol etc or whether you're taking a different path. I knew my only way out of the cultural restrictions was education. Buttershaw was a very rough school although in all fairness it's changing now. It's in the middle of an estate in one of the poorer parts of Bradford, a socially deprived area. You know at school my reports were saying I should have got straight As, but I never learnt the art of revision and I never did any homework because the environment just wasn't very supportive of you doing any work at home. You've got a family of seven kids and two parents, and you're all in a house and there's not a lot of peace and quiet and there's people arguing. My dad had had a heart attack when I was four and he was quite ill. I knew I had to work because the family situation was that we needed to.

At 16, I went to work in a bank and worked my way up. At 21, I had something like £25,000 in my bank account because I'd gone to work and hadn't spent any money at all. The money wasn't really mine even though it was in my account and I was earning it. It was for the contribution towards the family, and that was the understanding. My dad actually used to give me spending money, so I used to get £5 a week. I didn't have any expenses because I had no life! I used to go to work and come back and that was it. I actually did move out when I was 26, and not being thrown out and not on bad terms or anything like that. I was the youngest of seven, and the theory is that the eldest gets married first, so my three eldest brothers got married. My sister was fourth and she wasn't married, and neither were the others, so at that time there were still three people before me to get married, and I wasn't waiting around for them. I already had my mind set on what I wanted out of life. I still wasn't sure about how I was going to get it, but it certainly wasn't going to be marrying someone from back home.

I spoke to my dad and I said, "I'm 26 now and I need to have my own space and also think about my future. When you pass away, you can't guarantee that my brothers will look after me when I grow old, so I can't be living with them for the rest of my life." And my dad was like, "Actually, you're right!" At that time I didn't have any savings because my money had basically been used to buy a house in cash for one of my other brothers so he got his paid off and I got a mortgage.

After going home to a house which is packed with loads of people and then all of a sudden you're going home and the house isn't warm, and the heating's not been put on, and the food has not been prepared, sometimes that's a brilliant feeling because that's all you want, but there are times you can feel quite lonely. I actually still fasted at that time because it was about still having a bond with the family so I'd be ringing my brother, "What time does fast break today?" so there was still that communication, and

still having the thing in common with your family and with the rest of the Muslim society as well. So for quite a number of years I still fasted and then when I got to about 30 I was questioning what was I doing it for. I think the last couple of fasts were more a case of a weight watchers exercise. So it was for the wrong reasons anyway, not that I knew what the right reasons were in the first place because they weren't ever explained to me.

I think with not living with your immediate family you start to question. Do I pray? No, I don't. Do I believe there's a God? No, I don't. There's something but I wouldn't define it as God! But I appreciate my heritage which growing up it had more to do with culture rather than religion. Faith or concepts of God or why we did things wasn't really discussed. In terms of food, I still eat halal meat. I won't eat pork, I won't eat bacon, I won't eat anything that's not halal. I'm not religious but at this moment in time I just think I physically can't eat it. I've been conditioned so much that I think if I ate something else, I'd be sick. It's not a case of saying I was religious and then I stopped being religious. I don't think I was ever religious in the first place. If you don't have the fundamental belief growing up and all you've known is culture then you can't build a religion or a faith on that, and I never had the belief. I can't pretend to do or feel things that have never been nurtured. I get people saying that they will pray for me or get me a copy of the Quran in English. But what I find is that most people, like the over-50s Asian women I teach or my young practising Muslim students, they accept me for who I am. Sometimes you have to be honest with yourself and you just have to go through your own journey until something makes sense and roots you; it might go against how others do things and they might talk but at least you're being true to yourself and for the time being I find that what roots me is ju-jitsu.

I came across ju-jitsu by pure luck. I used to play badminton at Bradford College and this African man asked me if I wanted to try ju-jitsu. Every week that man kept asking me if I wanted to train, and then one day he said, "I'm not asking you anymore. You're a girl. You can't do it anyway." And that was the thing that I needed, and I got my socks and shoes off and went straight onto the mat. The first session I learnt to throw this big African man across the floor! Bearing in mind I was quite chubby because I hadn't done any exercise at all and I do like my food! The training was hard and I was doing it twice a week. I'd come home covered in bruises and I would ache, and my mum would say, "No one will attack you anyway. They'll think you've been attacked already!" I was a size 18 and I got right down to a size 10 in the space of six to eight months because I just think the fat was beaten out of me. After four years I got my black belt. It was comments like that and people saying things like "You will never make coach" that drove me, made me angry, and I was stubborn you know. I wanted to prove people wrong. If it wasn't for that man I don't think I would have achieved everything that I have — so I have a lot to be grateful for. Obesity is a huge issue in society, everywhere you look in Bradford you see burger joints and you can have all the adverts that you want but if governments don't invest in sports in schools or outside school then it's a problem. Kids used to play out a lot but there are so many fears now that parents don't want them going out unless it's organised and safe for them and that's what I try to provide.

I started training at the gym to get fitter because I was doing martial arts. I met my first partner there, a Muslim. I didn't even know how to flirt so for six months we were just exchanging hello's and a little bit of conversation. He'd not really had a girlfriend before so he was in exactly the same position as me. So I went to my parents and said, "Look, I actually came across somebody at the gym. He's asked me out to the cinema on a date." I was living in my own house so it wasn't like I was going to get kicked out of the house, but I still wanted that approval and their advice and guidance as well. What I didn't want was somebody seeing me with another man and coming back to my parents and saying, "Your daughter's a tart!" At this stage my dad knew that I was never going to have an arranged marriage and I think he was quite pleased that the person I did like was actually from a Muslim background as well. My mum was like, "Forget the date! We'll just go to his family and get you married. You don't need to go on a date. Why waste time?" My mum made it clear there was to be no sex before marriage and she spoke her mind very clearly.

Maybe in some ways I find my identity within ju–jitsu because there is no differentiation within religion or anything like that. The principal thing in ju–jitsu is that you show respect to everything and everyone, and that's the way I teach as well. Everybody's embraced and everybody's accepted. But my roots are still really important, not religious or Islamic roots, but

where you actually come from. I think about my family roots, like my dad telling me the story of when he first came over from Pakistan, and there was a house filled with about 10 or 15 men and they'd all share the rooms, working shifts in the factory – the hardship my dad went through. It's the journey about how you ended up being the person that you are now, and what your parents did, and who they are, that shape the person that you become. Your heritage and family history give you a sense of identity that you can relate to.

NEGARA KHATUN
JOURNEY TO THE HOUSE
OF ALLAH

*When My servants question you about Me, tell them that I am near. I answer
the prayer of every suppliant who calls to Me; therefore let them respond to Me,
and believe in Me. (Holy Quran: 2.186)*

OUR STORIES, OUR LIVES
NEGARA KHATUN

R ight now, for the first time I've fallen in love with my name, and last year or the year before or whenever, it was always Mina, Mina, Mina. It was about others. But now it's about me owning my name, my life, my choices and now I'm proud to say, "Yes, please do call me Negara Khatun."

I currently work in a school supporting children for whom English is a second language. I was born in Mombasa in Kenya in 1969. We lived in a really poverty stricken way. My (step) father, Abba Jee, has had the highest impact on my life, and he always said to me that, "Mina, all I could see was this woman with these five children, struggling." So yeah, he proposed to mum and they got married. I was seven years old when we emigrated to the UK, three sisters and two brothers. I was the youngest of all of them. After a bit of time in Nottingham, Abba Jee got a house in Percival Street in Bradford 3. It was a back to back property I think with only two bedrooms.

At that time, if you were a foreign student you were not sent straight to school. You were sent to language centres, but we were only there for a short while, because in Mombasa we were taught English in schools, so our English was fantastic. The point of these schools was to establish your English grammar. We were taught English grammar, we were taught basic English, and I think also it was nice. Speaking from my own experience, had I been thrown into a dominant white English-speaking different environment, where there were already routines and disciplines that you had to fall into – you know, it would have been quite scary as a foreign student because you're new to the country, you're new to the environment. Whereas the English centre was a very informal place. We had lessons and we had one thing in common – we were all new, not only to English but also to England. We were the real life version of the '80s comedy *Mind Your Language* – so many funny characters. We were from Africa, and there were some students from Pakistan, some from India, and some from other nationalities but it was a really nice family kind of an atmosphere. We were all supporting each other.

The schools at that time were all predominantly white and I had one Asian friend. We all had a crush on the same teacher, Mr Jackson, the music teacher. At that time we had a routine where we all knew as soon as the bell went, we had to queue up outside the classroom. We didn't have a seating plan so if you were earliest, you chose the best seats. Because it was Mr Jackson's lesson everybody wanted to be at the front. And five or 10 minutes before the bell, we'd be shooed away from the doorway because we'd start queuing up so early! Oh, he was so lovely that it never mattered to him if you sat at the front or sat at the back, you always got that special smile from him, and he always made you feel special! We all had a crush on him.

There was a lot of tension in the family, which brought disharmony throughout my childhood. I was quite tubby so I was bullied because I was the tallest and the broadest child in the class. I had a very inferior complex, that I was never going to be good enough for anybody, and if anybody bullied me, it was ok because I was bullied at home. I cried a lot when I was young. For a child, proper nurturing is very important. Love, affection, belonging, all these feelings have to take place for that child to have aspirations, for that child to want to think that they are able to become someone one day. I never had that! I grew up in a very lonely way. I had two sisters older than myself who got on very very well, and I never had anyone. For me the closest buddy was Abba Jee. I wanted to make Abba Jee proud of me, I remember that! I remember thinking he had done so much for us, and for him to have five children, some of whom were going through their teens and none of them were his!

There was quite clear racism in school, now we have a lot of race relations legislation that has helped but at that time no one cared whereas now it's more about religious discrimination really. Anyway, the school was in a predominantly white area. The students themselves, some would live and let live but some would make it quite explicit that you were in their territory and you were a wog. I remember one incident. Me and my brother at that time were in the same school. My brother was very much like myself – quiet and timid. We had to queue up for school dinners and we were already in a queue and the boys in the front didn't like that so they kept pushing him out, "You Paki! Go back to the queue!" And it escalated into a fight and they did hit him.

I mean, we were all called Paki names and wog names. It was new to us but I don't think any of us took it to the teachers. Don't forget our upbringing was very different. We were grateful that we were in this country. We thought, 'We've left a poor poor country and now we're in England, this rich country.' So you don't cause trouble and you don't attract trouble. It was the land of hope and glory! I don't know if we were just scared of having confrontations but we knew this was not our land. I knew England was a white country. So for me, whatever was given to me, I just thought, 'Well of course they're going to react like that. I'm in their country. Of course it's to be expected.' I felt like an intruder or I was made to feel like an intruder. You know, 'This is my territory. What are you doing here?'

Anyway, as a child back in Mombasa I was always eager to please. I was 13, happy go lucky. I'd just found my lovely figure because I'd lost weight, puppy fat all gone. And I was really enjoying school. And suddenly I came home and there were talks going on that this rishta had come for my big sister from Pakistan but that mum said yes for me. Our parents just thought these were their rights over their children. I thought it was time they were given a bit of happiness and I didn't want to disappoint them. I didn't want to hurt them. I don't know what the plans would have been but I knew I was too young, you know. So I told my mum, "What you've done I don't mind, but I'm not going to get married till I'm 18." I think because I didn't show any huge objection, the small pill that I did give mum, she swallowed quite happily. So at the age of 13 or 14, in my first year of secondary school, I was already spoken for!

As a 39-year-old now, I see this poor child engulfed in happiness that attention is being paid to her. She didn't realise those were her tender years. She could have been given the opportunity to become someone, become something. She never knew that life. Suddenly the importance of education was ripped away from her. She was gagged from a very young age. Education wasn't a priority now. There was nothing for me to do well in studies for! I was home, school, home, home, work, work, home, and then married. My husband came to England just before I was 18. He'd been very nice to me in Pakistan when I'd gone there for our engagement. You know, he shopped, he gave presents, and he stuck up for me when mum was yelling at me. And I found all of a sudden there was someone there who was willing to look after me, to protect me. It was really a nice feeling. I liked him and we'd spent time together. And when I came back, we wrote and exchanged letters and we were on the telephone for quite a while.

Although I was brought up in this country, I had my father's traditional values instilled, embedded in me to the core, because I'd shadowed him. He was like my friend. We would go to town, and on those trips, holding his hand, his rough hand, he would say, "Beta, money's not everything. Izzat is everything." He didn't know what he was doing, yet he was moulding me, teaching me about kindness, about respect, about not fighting back, about giving – that was life, you know. You didn't need to be loud and vulgar to be right. And if you have to forego your own happiness for the sake of someone else's, then that is the bigger happiness. So there I was from age eight till 17 or 18, shadowing my dad, being told all these beautiful, beautiful words. What values were really – real true values. So I knew instantly when I was going to get married, regardless of the fact that I was from this country and he was from back home, I had to be the good wife. I had to give myself more to please my husband. My pleasure was in pleasing my husband. His way was my way. Abba Jee had made me very mouldable, pliable, and don't forget, at 18 I'd still not seen the world, and there were no outside influences. So I was ready to lick and kiss and clean my husband's feet – that's the value that had been instilled in me. That was my role as a good wife.

I remember my husband was gobsmacked, that this was a 1980s bride, living in England, being brought up in the Western environment, and yet having all these Eastern, very traditional values. Even in Pakistan they would not do this anymore. I didn't even take my husband's name, you just referred to him as 'he' out of respect. But in my husband, as much as there was love, there was this horrible thing in him – possessiveness – "She is my possession. Anything she does outside, she cannot do without my permission! Anywhere she goes, anything she wears, she eats, she will do with my consent!" And it was my own fault. I fell into that so happily by becoming this humble wife, willing to please so much, and by not challenging him.

We had just been married 10 days and he smacked me. I cannot tell you how I felt at that time. I was a new bride and I had this hope of happiness. My mehndi was still on my hands. I was still being treated as a bride by everybody and there was my own husband, who I had brought into this country, in our bedroom, hitting me! That was the beginning of a very very awful start. All along, I just felt so lost. I was 18 and all of a sudden my life was taken away. I was married to what I thought was a very nice caring man, who turned out to be a split Jekyll and Hyde character. I don't even know what we argued over. He'd gag me and he used to hit me, push me, slap me around and I didn't retaliate because I didn't want anyone to find out. He kept crying, he kept pleading, he kept begging and promising, and whatever stupid things he did to win me back, it worked. I wanted my children to have both parents. You know, we may not be perfect but we're their parents. Now I had to be the good daughter as my father had taught me. It was now for me to put into practice all these so-called sacrifices that I was supposed to make. And you never know, maybe one day he'll wake up a different man – you know those stupid hopes I clung onto!

We were married for 15 years with many separations. It came to an end after many many years of stripping Abba Jee's old values. My survivor in all this was faith. Internally my faith was very strong, but I couldn't practise because I didn't have the peace of mind. I knew I read salat sometimes, but not regularly. I knew in Islam you're not allowed to hit a woman. I knew he was wrong, and I used to speak to Allah, "Allah, you created me, you're going to help me, don't desert me. I need so much strength." And gradually I came across a verse in the Quran that reads, 'Allah will not change your situation until you first change yourself.' I had to see that verse, I had to read that verse, I had to understand it, I had to feel it. I realised Allah is not going to come physically and take me out. No! I had to be responsible for myself. I had to stop being dependent on somebody else. I had to stop saying, "If my father says this then it must be right. If my husband says this, then that must be right." That was the beginning of Mina, who she is today. That was the time people began to see Mina in a different way. She realised Allah will help you, Allah will change you, but first take the initiative yourself. But I needed strength.

The strength came when he put a knife to my throat. For the first time, I looked at him and I said, "You want to strike that knife across my throat? Well do it! I'm sick of it. Day in, day out, you're threatening to kill me. If this is the way that Allah has written my life to end, then it will end, and I can do nothing to protect myself because it has been written that way." And God knows, he didn't do it. He couldn't. He threw the knife and walked out. And I called the police and that was it.

He said two things in my marriage that made me understand why he became what he became. He already had a friend here that he knew from Pakistan, who'd got married to a girl from here. And in the early days, he told my husband that all these British Pakistani girls, they're all whores, and the only reason their parents get them married from back home is that they can't find a decent man here. "So don't trust your wife, no matter how good she's making out she is; she must be a whore." And my husband lived in agony believing this. And the day he finally left in 2004, he goes, "Mina, look at yourself! I'm leaving but I'm leaving you the way I wanted. You're a young woman with five children. Who will have you now? If I can't have you, nobody will have you!"

Domestic violence is a crime that any woman can suffer at the hands of; it has nothing to do with class or faith or profession. And it's not just physical, it's mental, emotional and psychological and the impact it has on children is incredible. It's something that can never be justified and no community can ever overlook it because where it exists no community can prosper. I do not consider myself a victim anymore. I am far from it. I like the woman that looks back at me in the mirror. I like the woman that works and gives back to the community. I like the woman that brings her children up and encourages them and loves them. But this confidence came with time. I had to rebuild spiritually. I had to give back to Allah now because Allah was my shadow now. He was with me. Allah asks from us to follow Islam, not just by name, not just by lip service. There are five fundamental pillars of Islam and two of them are compulsory. You're not a Muslim until you've said your Shahada and you're not a Muslim until you pray. And that guilt was eating me up. I had to start giving. I had to start praying now. I had to become a Muslim with my actions.

Two years on, I had a bit of money and we were able to afford a family holiday. One of my daughters said, "I think we should go for Umrah. If we're going to go anywhere, what is a better place to go than the house of Allah?" I was personally going there just to say thank you to Allah. I wanted to go to Allah with a clean slate, and not to take anyone's grudge with me. It wasn't a place where you take little grudges and anger. For me, it was about going there and saying, "Allah, thank you! Even for the hard times!" Because through those hard times I was being remoulded and strengthened. Had I remained the passive and submissive Mina, I would never be here today. So I wanted to go to Umrah, to walk the streets of

Madina and to know our Prophet had walked through these streets, to pray in the Masjid Nabvi where our Prophet is buried. Just to be in that air!

My parents wanted me to be like them, to live in their values, to live in their beliefs. We lived our parents' lives. I don't want that for my children. My mum and dad didn't let me go out – "Girls don't go out, girls don't do this, girls don't do that." Now for me that's very cultural. Islam doesn't differentiate. The Quran addresses the 'believing man' and the 'believing woman', so for me if my son is a believing man and my daughter is a believing woman, then the law is the same for them both. My daughters have the same rights as their brothers as far as education and marriage are concerned. My daughters have got aims, they've got goals, they've got aspirations. They value themselves. They're strong and they're articulate. I instil in my daughters the right of respect from everyone, and that respect means love. I've instilled the fact that they have rights as individuals, that I have to meet as a parent – the right of a good home, the right of education, the right of meeting their happiness.

Rejwana Malik
I have a Dream!

I have a dream that my four children will one day live in a nation where they will not be judged by the colour of their skin but by the content of their character.
(Martin Luther King)

I got my A'level results recently and achieved two As and a B and now I'm at uni. I attended Feversham Islamic College for seven years. It's an all girls' school; I was 11 when I started there. Academically I think all the girls in that school do well.

A lot of people assume that going to Feversham College means all the girls are narrow minded or they won't really socialise with other people, but we do mix in with different people. We're respectful towards what they believe and what they practise. I do know that sometimes people think that just because a school is faith based that it's somehow going to be extremist, people look at places like Saudi Arabia, Afghanistan and Iran and think those sorts of things. My experiences, as a young woman born in Britain, is completely different to the experiences of woman in other countries – it's unique to this country. I just get sick of people comparing us to Muslim women in third world countries! Who is the one with the narrow mind I ask you? – I'm just like any other teenager – but I'm Muslim – simple as!

It's nice to get to know other people's backgrounds and their culture. I have diverse friends from different nationalities and some of them are non-Muslims. One's French, one's Pakistani, another Gujarati. So the things that we do are mixed. Sometimes we go to an Asian restaurant like Ambala's or Sunrise and other times we'll go to McDonald's. The school used to be very small, with maybe a couple of hundred students. Now that they've made a bigger building, it's about 600 and still rising. All the teachers there are really cool basically. What's a bit surprising to other people is they'll expect all the teachers to be Muslims and actually the majority I think are white and non-Muslim and even the head teacher is a non-Muslim. I think what they're trying to show is that we're welcoming white people, non-Muslims too, that they can lead and coordinate a school, and it doesn't matter if they're non-Muslims. The head teacher has to do everything the head of another school has to do, but in our school, they respect the rules that are laid down. It's the same as every other school.

At school I was always into sport. I love sport! I support Liverpool by the way and my favourite player is Steven Gerrard. I like to know where Liverpool is in the league table, how they're doing and their history. I've been playing football for as long as I can remember – at primary school, six a side, nine a side, lots of tournaments. In Feversham I was a sports leader and have a leadership qualification. I wouldn't mind playing for the Liverpool Girls' Team but I don't know what my dad would say (maybe I do I just don't want to think about it!). At this time he would not approve because obviously they run around in shorts and he would not approve of that, especially now I'm older. It does sound a bit funny when you walk down the street and someone says, "She can play football or she can kick a ball" and others are going, "Yeah right, she's a girl in a jilbab. What can she do!"

We're Bangladeshi and we're quite a strict religious family. My dad's quite well known within the Bangladeshi community and if you live in a small community, they tend to talk! What our parents would say and what we'd say is different at times. Our thinking differs because obviously some of the parents that came to England at the beginning they were taught back at home and we've had a Western education. It puts pressure on you when you're compared to other people. That's typical among Asians – you know how your parents might compare you to one of your cousins who may be achieving higher or dressing in a certain way? I've got four younger brothers all under the age of 10. Two of my brothers are doing hifz, they're memorising Quran. They will have achieved so much at such a young age and me and my sister are older and we're like, "what have we done?" In the eyes of most parents secular knowledge isn't valued as much as religious to be honest. But I'm at university and I will have a degree in a few years time – the first girl in the family! In our case, we want to go to university. We're modernised in terms of how we practise Islam – it's about getting the balance right so upholding the key tenants of our faith, having values and respecting them. I also want to go out there and work and help other people – there are so many more women than men excelling in education I think we will start to take on roles that we haven't taken on before, in Parliament, as peace activists, pioneers in health, business and fashion and I have my own ambitions and dreams.

I'm quite a whacky person with really eclectic tastes. I used to listen to music but right now I'm into Japanese and Korean culture. I absolutely love that culture – anything to do with the Japanese, Korean or Taiwanese. I watch their dramas on the internet and it's really interesting. They all have morals to each of their dramas and it really makes you think, 'Wow! They're full of wisdom.' At first they sounded weird, you know speaking in their language, but with the subtitles on, I'm used to it now. I watch my dramas on the internet because you can't get them on the TV. I find *Eastenders* such a bore and these dramas are so much more interesting. I don't like watching the Indian films because they're far too cheesy and predictable. With the Japanese dramas, there's always a moral. I learn off the dramas. You know with soaps like *Emmerdale* and *Eastenders*, they're really Western so everything they do is a bit exposed, something that Asians might find a bit too offputting. But then again you have lots of satellite channels now. People have got alternative entertainment like the dramas and news. My dad used to tell me that there was a time there were only two or four channels. There is so much choice now and if something happens in the news people watch more than one channel to get the bigger picture because some channels can be really biased.

Dress is always mentioned where Muslim women are concerned. How comfortable you feel depends on how you wear your hijab really. It depends what material you're wearing. Silk ones, they just slide off – annoying! Cotton ones are ok. I try to do it the Turkish style where you have to wrap it around you're head but it takes ages for me. I take a long time. Everything else I put on quickly but my hijab takes the longest. Obviously if you weren't wearing the hijab, naturally girls would want their hair straightened or curled or nicely done, so the same thing really applies to hijab. If you're going to wear hijab you at least make yourself look nice. You want to be happy in it and comfortable in it, so I take my time before I go out, to make sure there's no creases or folds or anything like that. I've been wearing the hijab ever since I attended Feversham. It's part of the uniform and my parents thought it was time for me to wear it, and I believed it was time for me to wear it as well. The uniforms differ according to what year you're in. Year 7 to Year 11, they wear navy hijab and navy shalwar kameez. And the sixth formers have to wear black hijab and a navy jilbab. It's a must. You have to wear it. But 50 or 60% of the girls don't wear hijab outside school. But I do get called names like "ninja" or people jokingly call me "sister, sister" or "Woaah she's holy – be careful of what you says." It's like you're a UFO – an 'unidentified funny object' not an 'unidentified flying object – LoL' – you have to laugh … not at me though!

I still wear my hijab when I go to celebrate a wedding. Basically we put on those heavily jazzed-out scarves, those long scarves with sequins on or beads on and we attend weddings in them, like with a matching scarf. But the scarves are not plain or anything. They're really thickly beaded, there's Indian patterns on them and everything and we wear matching broaches and bangles and stuff to go with it. So you see you can still wear your hijab and jilbab and look flashy and look like it's an occasion. I go to Bombay Stores. Even if you think there's not going to be something there, you still have to check because it's a huge store, it's well known and they're getting in new clothes regularly like hijabs and stuff. There might be something that you might like or something that's on sale. But now, my friend has opened her own jilbab business so she makes all my jilbabs for me. She makes them the way I like it. So basically me and her go to Fabric Hut down Toller Lane. I like that place. It sells a lot of nice fabrics. I get most of my fabrics from there, all different colours and matching hijabs with it. So she's sewed me loads of jilbabs that I'll be wearing to university. You know you have your plain jilbab and then you can put another layer on top so it's like more like a dress. If I do buy a jilbab, depending on what colour it is, I probably have to get a matching hoodie with it, you know like a sleeveless thingy that you can wear on top of your jilbab instead of wearing a jacket or something. It looks a bit sporty as well. When I go to university, I don't want to look plain compared to everybody else because it will be non-Muslims and white people around, and they'll be wearing their casual clothes and they'll be jazzed out. So if I'm going to wear jilbab, I don't want to look dull, like someone who's just come from a funeral – LOL!

When people come across Me a Muslim – I don't want them to associate me with 7/7 or 9/11, Osama bin Laden or Saddam Hussein but pictures of the blue mosque, the fragrances of morocco, date palms in Egypt or the Taj Mahal. Then we will have succeeded!!

SOFIA MASKIN
FROM ROOTS TO ROUTES

It is really a wonder that I haven't dropped all my ideals, because they seem so absurd and impossible to carry out. Yet I keep them, because in spite of everything I still believe that people are really good at heart. (Anne Frank)

A week before my seventh birthday in England we went to Pakistan. My dad had a real desire to go back to his mother land. Like most of the first generation he left behind most of his loved ones and came out of a village first time on an aeroplane to an alien country that was cold, wet, snowy and unwelcoming. Now we see the Eastern Europeans going through a similar sort of process the only difference is they're used to the bad weather!

My father came here when he was fairly young and he felt like he missed out on a lot so he wanted to go back and live the moments he didn't have but this time with all of us there. My brother didn't take to it so they sent him back to Bradford where he lived with my grandparents, my uncles and auntie. For me it was a real adventure being in a completely different country, the hot climate, school life and just being able to roam around freely in the village. People grew their own crops, tended to the animals, milked cows far more relaxed compared to all the running around I do here at home. The school I went to was fairly traditional in the sense we didn't have calculators and had to do a lot of reading and memorisation. The downside was me missing out on primary school back here in the UK but I didn't fair badly when I came back and I'm currently working in an art gallery because I have an arts background, textiles and design. To be honest I think that experience of going back home put that tiny spark inside me that made me want to travel to see things outside little Bradford, you know other parts of the UK and the world. Four years later my dad decided to come back. My parents chose to live with my grandparents although we had our own house but we just didn't live there. I think part of the reason was so we could have time to adjust back into this country without having to worry about sorting the house out and having six kids it helps having extra pairs of hands to help out. I think if it was up to my grandma, we'd still be living with them!

Obviously when you're younger you don't have this notion of space or that we're going to have a bedroom each. So as a child, my grandmother's house seemed huge to me. It was a Victorian terrace house. It had five bedrooms, also had a living and a front room and it had two cellars – one of them we converted into like a kitchen and sitting room area. I never had my own bedroom. If you don't know what having your own bedroom is like, then you make do. As well as my own family being fairly big I have a large extended family – that I value. I remember as a child on the weekends, all my cousins, my other aunties and their kids used to come over and fill my grandparents' house. It just seemed like we had lots of space. And even now, on Eid and family occasions, when we all want to sleep over at whoever's house, you make do. You'll just put a mattress on the floor and we'll all just camp out. You don't care about that comfort. You care more about the company. Nowadays I look at society and that same sense of valuing family is not there.

Growing up I went through all sorts of phases that made me ask questions about identity, where I was going in life, why I dressed the way I did, and all that sort of stuff. I still do! I used to wear my scarf on my head the Pakistani way – thrown on with half the hair covered and if the wind was blowing then none – I wouldn't call it the hijab – you wear it because you've been doing it since whatever age. I guess it's because you are imitating the women around you who might not necessarily be religious but it's very much part of their culture and in some cases maybe their understanding of Islam. I saw it as just another part of the outfit, the shalwar/kameez that everyone wore – I remember my mum used to say to me when I was younger, "If you're wearing it, wear it properly," and I used to think, 'What is wearing it properly?' I remember sitting on a bus on my way to university and there was a girl sitting next to me who I sort of knew. She was doing her Arabic degree at Leeds. She was a practising Muslim and she wore the hijab. She was a really sweet lass. We were chatting away, and I don't know how but we got onto the topic of aunties and uncles; your aunt's husband and the level of purdah you should have in front of people. We were chatting about that and she just said, "You know that you don't have a choice." She was talking about the hijab. And her words just made me think. I suppose I always knew that you have to wear it but I never took that step. I had looked into it previously and reached the understanding it was a command from God and if I wanted to live my life a certain way then I would have to wear it but it's a step no one can force you to take and that was the case with me. But by her just uttering those few words I thought, 'Yeah, she's right.' And I remember coming back that evening and trying it on properly and trying to cover all my hair, and trying to wear it in different ways. And that's it; next morning I just wore it. I think people looked at me but not like, "Ooh she's wearing the hijab." I think I was half way there with the dupatta, and so it just came on. And it's never come off. And now, I definitely feel bare if I don't wear it. It's just part of me. I've got friends and cousins that will come home and they'll rip their hijabs off in the comfort of their homes and take their scrunchies off because they need to let their hair down. But for me, it stays on until I go to bed. I see the hijab as an honour for women, a protection through a simple garment. For me it's also a symbol that shows others I am a Muslim which is really important to me and recently I was talking to a friend and she summed it up beautifully by saying, "It's a public declaration of a very private intention." I guess you can draw the analogy with a wedding ring which people have come to accept. It's very much a part of me now.

I get asked a lot of questions about identity when I travel and I enjoy travelling! It doesn't matter where the road takes me. I'm lucky to have a really tight group of friends. Most of them happen to be young, single, professional women – and we all have a sense of humour. It's not that typical image you get of a very serious Muslim woman that's incapable of having a laugh. As you grow older you realise the importance of that expression 'you are the company you keep'. We all have that get up and go to explore the world especially the Muslim world – it just opens your eyes and your heart up to the bigger picture – there's more beyond Bradford, we have a rich creative and architectural heritage in places like Spain and I just want to experience all that amazing richness and contribute towards creating a same sense of that incredible beauty. In the past it was never the norm to travel to other countries besides Pakistan but that's all changing now. I feel I've been put here to contribute and not drain society and I see more and more women doing just that. The Muslim world is not exactly heaving with tourists and you know that 'stay away' image we get doesn't exactly help but that hasn't stopped me. More and more women are gaining knowledge, not just following a blind faith or accepting what others are telling them – it's actually about going out there and searching and finding out things for yourself.

I'm finding that as my interest and knowledge in my faith grows my life and travel choices seem to be navigated by the scholars I admire and look up to. I remember not long ago I attended a lecture by a Syrian scholar, Sheikh Mohammad Yaqoobi, in Keighley and he was talking about one of his teachers back in Damascus and it sparked an interest for me to visit the place and so I did ... sometimes it takes a simple thing like that to make me wanna get up and go and I'm lucky enough to do that.... Some people look up to traditional Pakistani scholars or go to gatherings where they speak Urdu and that kind of thing. But I think in English and look up to figures like Imam Zahid Shakir and Sheikh Hamza Yusuf, American convert scholars, who have studied in lots of Muslim institutions around the world – one of them being in Morocco. I've been there twice and it left me wanting to learn more so the following year off we went again – lonely planet guide in hand! It's funny because when you travel to various places armed with the Yorkshire accent – people find it difficult to comprehend it; firstly because you're a group of Muslim women travelling on your own and secondly that you're British. It happened to me in New Zealand when I was sat in a park with a friend and someone approached us and asked where we were from. And I remember when I went to Poland and the Lord Mayor said, "Why haven't you got English names?" and I said, "Our names come from the Arabic or Persian language." That always gives people food for thought. I think we live in an age and a world right now where people are curious about Muslims so we have to be open and not defensive. At the same time I've got so much to learn from other people, places, civilisations. For example, there's so much as a Muslim community we have to learn from other communities like the Jewish community in the UK, the way they organise themselves and support their young people to excel. It's not just a one-way thing – it has to work both ways!

To be honest, I think I'm far more politically aware than I've ever been before. I remember when we stopped off in Palestine/Israel on our way to Mecca Saudi Arabia. Apart from being stopped at the border between Jordan and Israel for 10 hours I had an incredible experience. There are loads of people who see the injustice and apartheid and we'll see if things change with the election of Barack Hussein Obama. Most people want to see peace in that place, you only have to look at all the marches on the capitals around the world to know that. At the same time it's sacred to all three of the world's major religions, strange how you have the mosques, synagogues and churches all in close proximity – you hear the bells and call to prayer one after the other. Knowing that I followed in the footsteps of the Prophets in this Holy Land is mind blowing – I never thought that I would achieve that goal, never thought that I would ever walk down the narrow streets of the Old City, smiling at the Palestinian women with their multi-coloured jilbabs, or the Orthodox Christians with their shiny golden crosses or see the Jews racing towards the Western Wall. Each of us is connected by a really profound and enriching historical past; it unifies us but also sadly divides us. It's so tragic when you think about it.

I think when you go to places like Palestine you really do appreciate the freedom you have in the UK, the freedom to move freely, the freedom to talk to whoever you want, eat what you want, have access to water, electricity – a home – those sorts of things. It's home! Most professional Muslim women I see around me – are financially independent, educated, highly organised and media savvy; we travel, within and outside of the UK and we're very culturally and politically aware. As for work it's more than just the pay packet at the end of the month – it's something I believe in because I want to contribute, give back to my community, black and white, Muslim or not. I don't think you would see me sat in one place for longer than five minutes! I always loved the arts – we need all of that stuff right now with the world in economic crises, employment at an all-time low and the credit crunch and all; put a smile on people's faces. Being creative means I'm around creative people and luckily my work is all about making a positive difference to others – especially young people from Bradford who just need a break!

SYIMA MERALI
JIHAD

The worries of the world burden me greatly, and from them I wish to part. Then I can live in solitude while the thorns of sadness leave my heart. These birds who sit in the tree singing all day long.... Their chirping is beautiful and will be my song.... O Allah! Let my cry make all those empathetic hearts ache, And the ones who are unconscious or indifferent, awake. (Allama Iqbal)

Y ou know how sometimes you read and you read, and you've got all of this information that's just sat there, and then you read one thing, and it sort of puts it all together? Well, that's how I found my faith. For me, that was about seven or eight years ago. Before that there were times when I thought that there was a God out there and there were other times that I thought no, there's no God! This is all rubbish. There were times when I'd do my prayers and times when I didn't. I couldn't just really believe because it had to be there intellectually.

It was important that I was able to make a connection between what I had in my head and in my heart. I didn't want to simply do things because people told me to do them or because I wanted to please others. I think it's far too easy to go down that road. People like things to be ordered and anyone that questions or reflects critically and questions norms can become an outcast but that isn't being true to yourself. Before that, I wanted to believe and at times it made sense to me, and at other times it didn't. I started wearing the hijab post 9/11 but I had been thinking about it before. I think people may have perceived that 9/11 played a part in that but in all honesty, it didn't! After I started wearing hijab, my mum went to Pakistan and one of my cousins asked how I was and my mum said, "Oh yes, she's started wearing the hijab!" and the reaction she got was "But she's quite nice looking! Why is she wearing the hijab?" I thought that was really funny – "Ok! Only ugly girls wear it then!"

When the whole faith thing clicked for me, I thought the hijab was a requirement. The other thing is my family, sect wise, we're a mixture, some of us are Sunni and some are Shia. I'm Sunni and my husband is Shia. And we've always gone to the Muharram gatherings – sometimes speakers are really good other times you cringe because their perspectives on the role of women in today's society are extremely poor. As for the mosques they've opened up spaces for women and I've heard that one or two women have taken up positions on mosque committees but more needs to be done to make it a space that's welcoming. One of the emotive historical examples that you hear about during these gatherings concerns the hijab and its symbolic importance. After the great massacre at Kerbala located in present-day Iraq in which the grandson of the Prophet was massacred, women had their scarves taken away and they were marched bear headed from Kerbala to Kufa, and then on to Damascus. In doing this they were trying to publicly disgrace them, take away their dignity and cause humiliation. For me, in Islamic history, Karbala is one of the most inspiring events, and that for me was one of the big inspirations for wearing the hijab. You know you get these eulogies and lamentations that surround the events of Karbala, well I always make a point during the period of Muharram to try not to listen to songs, but listen to these instead. And I thought, 'Oh my God! I'm a complete contradiction in terms!' because I'd be there in my nice company car with my hair all nicely done, in my suit, and I'd be listening to these eulogies about these women who'd had their headscarves taken!

I thought about wearing the hijab a good year and a half or two years before I actually put it on. My background is sales, marketing and account management and I was in a client facing role and I really thought this would be a boulder in terms of career progression. That was really the only thing stopping me. In the kind of job that I was doing there were not many Asian people working in the company and certainly not people wearing hijab. The perception around hijab is very negative and people do stereotype. It's not just English people who stereotype, it's Asian people as well. I find it quite funny now that I do wear the hijab, apart from the people that know me, others have this perception that I must have had an arranged marriage or that I must be very submissive, and that isn't the case – it's far from it in fact. I think in the workplace, those stereotypes are still out there. Before I started wearing the hijab, I was the Asian girl but I was fun and outgoing and I fitted in. But all of a sudden, it was like I was an unknown quantity because I was seen as one of the group, so I think people found it quite strange. Then I used to think, 'Well, I'll have a child and I'll stop working and then I'll wear it.' But then I thought, 'Well, actually that's a real cop out! That's me doing it when it's easy for me, but I won't do it if it's difficult for me.' I had a chat with my boss about it. We'd actually been somewhere and I'd been toying with the idea of asking him, and as we were walking up the stairs to the office, I just said, "Neil, how would you feel if I covered my hair?" And he said, "What do you mean? With gel?" And I said, "No, with a scarf!" He did get the concept. He knew what I was talking about so we had a chat and I said, "Look I'd like to do this. Would it be a problem for you guys because obviously when you employed me, I wasn't wearing it. This is my decision and I don't want to force it upon you guys if it's an issue for you. I'm not going to take you to an employment tribunal or anything like that." A lot of people did ask me, "Are you wearing it because you're

about to get married?" And I said, "No, I've been married for four years."
It's amazing how people feel it can't have been your own decision. You
must be doing it because you've been asked to or told to or whatever, and
the fact that you might choose to do this voluntary doesn't seem to occur
to people. I know now that hijab is becoming a bit of a fashion accessory
but I've never seen the hjiab in that way. I feel that the emphasis in Islam
about the greater struggle was important, the struggle against the self, and
for me putting on the hijab in the workplace when I felt it was probably
going to damage my career prospects was part of the struggle.

Previously I don't think I ever felt good enough. I didn't feel I was
practising enough; I wasn't regular enough with my prayers so therefore I
wasn't ready to wear it. And I got to the point where I thought, 'Actually,
life is a struggle, it's never perfect, you are never perfect.' And for me to
think I was going to reach some kind of spiritual nirvana before I was
going to put the hijab on, then that was probably never going to happen.
And I felt with wearing the hijab it made me more careful of what I was
saying, of what I was doing, because I think once you do put the hijab on,
people have certain perceptions of you. People know you're a Muslim.
Without the hijab, you could be any number of things and therefore the
way you behave is actually quite important because then it's a label for
other Muslims.

I've been wearing it for quite a long time now, but over the last couple
of months, I've actually thought about taking it off and at one point I got
really close to taking it off. We opened the restaurant nearly three years
ago now and last year we put alcohol in. We were in the position where
either we let the business go or it needs alcohol putting in. It was about
to crash and burn and we made that decision – you know you think,
'I know it's wrong but I'm going to do this.' I can't afford to suffer the
consequences of the business going. The premises have to be licensed and
there has to be one person in the restaurant who has a personal licence
to serve alcohol. I hold the licence for this place and you have to do an
exam too, and the day I went to do that was very difficult for me. The day
I went to do that I was thinking, 'What am I doing? What have I done
with my life?' And on the way there I listened to this CD I have called
'Reflections on Surat al Bakara' by Sheikh Hamza Yusuf. In it he talks
about how we don't have the faith of angels and our belief is not perfect
and that made me feel a bit better.

Selling alcohol for me was very much a turn around on a principle. It wasn't something I wanted to do and I sort of felt if I was running a business where I was serving alcohol, should I really be wearing the hijab? I felt it was a contradiction and I had quite a funny day where we had some customers in very late. I was very tired so I sat on the bar – the ledge – and I was nodding off. And I just thought, 'This must look so strange! I'm sat here in a hijab with these bottles of alcohol behind me!' I felt that when I'd put it on, I had all these aspirations and I wanted to do certain things. I'd started an Islamic Studies degree. I was doing things that I was happy with. I thought I was trying to develop myself in the right direction and now I felt I wasn't doing that anymore. I felt, 'Does it really reflect me anymore?' So I had quite a big struggle over it. I sort of felt if I'd had enough faith, if I had the level of faith that I should or that I aspire to, then I would have said, "Tawaqqal il lila, I will rely on God and God will provide and something will work out." But I didn't. I said, "Oh my God, I will put alcohol in!"

I got to the stage where I thought life is not a straight line and we end up in situations in life that you can't predict. Then I thought there are a lot of things in life in which I'm not perfect and there are so many areas of my belief which are imperfect, and I felt if I was to take off the hijab it would be the last thing. I felt I'd lose it all completely.

I think because I was wearing hijab people felt they were able to say to me, "Why are you doing this?" I still get this where people come up to pay and they'll say, "Sister, do you realise that if you serve alcohol, it makes your earnings haram, that your earnings are tainted?" I would never ever say that serving alcohol is right because I don't personally believe it to be so. I wouldn't say that my earnings are untainted because I believe them to be tainted, and I didn't want them to be tainted in that way. However, what I hope is that God realises why I did what I did and what my intentions were, and just how hard I did struggle to make the business work without the alcohol, and it didn't. I just thought, 'Well I'm doing things that are wrong but it doesn't make me an unbeliever.' I think the hijab is a part of things, it's not everything. It's not your faith in its totality. And in the end, I didn't want to lose my hijab.

I suppose my life has been full of challenges, none more so than when I was told that I had cancer. But I've never been one to run away from challenges. I suppose there are some things that you simply have to confront in a very pragmatic way. You have no choice!

I was diagnosed with breast cancer when my daughter was a year and three quarters. My mind was on fast forward; I was reflecting and questioning a great deal. Quite soon after I was diagnosed, somebody died and I went to the mosque for the funeral, and I did think, 'That could be me' – you know the whole coffin thing and the grave; people praying and crying over your coffin – my mum, my husband, my daughter and all that. I didn't particularly see myself as a good, pious sort of person. It did make me think, if in three weeks' time they say, "That's it", what have I actually done with my life? I thought, 'Realistically as a person, where am I? What have I done about my spirituality, about my own self-development, about making myself a better person?' And that's why the whole alcohol thing was like turning the other way from all of this. You don't think you're going to die, do you? We just think we've got all the time in the world to sort ourselves out and be better people and all that kind of stuff. When you think about it our time on this beautiful planet is so short – it begs the question, how are we choosing to live our daily lives? What are we actually contributing?

Something like that does make you realise just how precarious life really is, that in a single incident everything can change. We make all these long-term plans and you don't take into account that the one thing that underpins all of them is actually our life, which is something we have no control over. But then you're also aware that people die and it's a tragedy and yet life carries on. None of us are indispensable! None of us are greater than the entire picture. The world doesn't actually stop for anyone, and no matter what happens to you, life still carries on.

When I first found out they said we don't know what your long-term future is. I begged God for time to bring my daughter up. I was very very worried about my daughter – she was very young at the time. I did think I'll write things down for her, things for her to know, things that she should think about. I had this real horror of her being brought up by somebody else. The most horrible thing for me was that I thought she won't remember me because she is so young. If I actually die now, she won't even have a memory of me. It'll just be photographs. That was quite hard because she is so central to me. And I suppose when you have a child you have all these aspirations about what you want to be with them, what you want to do together, and places that you might want to visit. Like she'll get married, I won't be there or when she goes to senior school or when she's having exams. I'd thought when she's a bit older I'll take her to The Louvre in Paris and what I'll read to her. But again I have no control over the length of my life and that prospect is humbling on the one hand and very scary and dehumanising on the other. One of the first things I did when I was diagnosed was I bought the complete set of the Narnia books. I was a big fan because I'd read them growing up and I didn't have all of them, and I thought it might not occur to somebody else. So I bought them for her because I thought, at least if I'm not around, at least she'll read them….!

UMM MOHSIN
The Preacher's Voice

*If nature has made you a giver, your hands are born open, and so is your heart.
And though there may be times when your hands are empty, your heart is
always full, and you can give things out of that. (Frances Hodgson Burnett)*

My name is Umm Mohsin and I am an aalima. My parents are from Gujarat in India. I think with the Pakistani community something that always touches me is despite whatever happens within them, they're very close compared to the Gujaratis. We're not that close. What I see with the Pakistanis is regular trips to Pakistan. With Gujaratis I think that has drifted away.

I come from a very large family – of several sisters and two brothers. I was born in Yorkshire. My father was working in a factory as a welder and mum was a housewife. I went to primary school to the age of 10, then alongside my older sisters, I went to India to study the aalima course. That was actually the first boarding place of its kind in the world at that time and it's been running over 40 years now. I really don't know how my father afforded it but I really think it was the barkat of his halal income. He was working so hard and I'm sure they struggled. I stayed there for five years and I didn't come home in between. Some of my older sisters did not study further but the rest of us all attended boarding school. I remember the first time that I went to the school. It was midnight, pretty dark. We were offered some food which was yogurt curry and fried roti. I had to sleep in the communal hall – everyone slept on the floor – as I picked up my pillow I remember I saw a little cockroach underneath it and screamed. And that was my first experience at the boarding school.

After I graduated in 1988, after five years of study, I came back home. I was wearing full burkha by then but I didn't have the confidence of going out with my burkha. I'd been wearing it in India but I wasn't used to seeing so many non-Muslims around. The village that we studied in, everybody wore their burkha whether they covered their face or not. I guess over time it had become more of a cultural thing for them where any woman you'd see, even if she was going down to the next street to her mum's house, she'd put on the full burkha, so you didn't feel alienated by wearing it.

Coming back to England, I remember an incident when I must have been about seven, before going to study. I wasn't in burkha of course. My mum used to wear the burkha. I remember going into town with mum and a couple of white lads threw a bottle of alcohol on mum, and that just stayed with me for a very long time. I remember thinking, 'What if that happens to me!' That was something that I'd gone away with. And now

I'd come back, although mum was wearing the burkha and there was the odd few others that were wearing the burkha. Initially it actually took my dad's support to say, "You need to get into town. I'm getting old. I can't bring home the shopping. You're going to have to go!" That was the line he would use. That was his way of supporting me and pushing me out into the community and gaining that confidence. I did lack a lot of confidence. These sorts of supportive comments helped me to be proud of what I had and being happy about what I was wearing and what I was doing.

So if I was to say I'm an aalima, in a very broad sense that means I have learnt about Islam. I've actually learnt to understand Arabic, and that is the Quranic classic Arabic, not the modern Arabic, although it's very easy for me now to latch on to the modern Arabic. I've also been taught the translation of the Quran. Then moving on, I've studied the books of the sayings of the Prophet (peace and blessings be upon Him). Also I've studied Islamic jurisprudence which is known as Fiqh, how to conduct your day-to-day life etc. If you were to ask me a question, if I don't have the answer, then I'll look it up and if I don't get the answer from the books then I'm going to have to refer to somebody who's much more knowledgeable than myself.

My husband's an aalim and I'm the female equivalent. The only thing is we, as women, don't lead the prayers. He's in the same position where he's had people ringing him for advice or where they've needed help. I think apart from the salat leading, I've actually joined him with everything he does, so we have a lot in common. There is such a need for alimas in society right now. I am finding that more and more women want to consult an authority for decisions – they are independent and want to find answers for themselves. Women are thirsty for knowledge and they will bypass institutions that don't cater for their needs in order to quench that thirst so if it means organising themselves in their homes they will.

As an aalim or aalima you're qualified to actually teach the subjects that you've studied yourself. I have a circle of women where we get together just for an hour a week, and I will either read one of the sayings of the Prophet (peace and blessings be upon Him) or depending on the time of the year, if it's Ramadan, I will cover Ramadan topics. If it's Eid ul Adha time, I will cover the subject of sacrificing animals, the essence of Eid and things like that. I'm finding that more and more women want to learn and the safest and best places seem to be in each other's homes. They commit themselves, find others who can look after their children and they come and learn. It's a very very open discussion we have, where the women see me as the main teacher but at the same time the class is very informal where mothers with little children can come along as well. We'll have the toys there on one side so they can play. Sometimes I can hardly hear myself because there's so many children. And nobody's obliged to come once and then come every week. From within that class, there's one woman who's actually turned to me because of problems with her sister-in-law where she feels anything she says is going against her, and she will actually ring me if she's feeling down. There's one sister who herself is very practising but doesn't have a very practising partner. She feels that sometimes she just needs to talk to somebody, somebody she can relate to – an ear – a support. Sometimes it's women contacted me with regards to reading salat or if they have irregular periods which affects their prayers, because you can't read when you are on your periods. These sorts of issues. I had a lady knocking at the door and she said, "I need to learn how to read my Quran better. Even if you could give me half an hour to listen to my Quran." So women are desperate to learn about their faith – we can't assume that just because an individual is a Muslim that they are practising or that they will be able to read or understand the Quran.

There's some sisters that turn up. I've been there with quite a few of them when they've said the Shahada – the first step of becoming a Muslim. I go through the kalima, translate it and make sure they understand it, and the basic fundamental beliefs of Islam. I go through what it actually means, what the implications are, so by the time it comes to them reading it, they're fully aware of what they're actually saying, and they're not coming into something blindly. Then, depending on if they've already got help on learning more about Islam, I either leave that to them or I leave them my number in case they need more help. Some women come wanting to learn more about Islam, and if that's the case, I guide them to books to study, and see how they feel about it, and may encourage them to get in touch with other scholars.

Sometimes the choice to turn to Islam has been only for marriage purposes. I'll be honest, and I've actually said to them, when it comes to Islam, it's actually got to be for the right reasons. "You can't simply accept

Islam for the sake of getting married, and then forget what you've actually done. It's got to be something from deep within that you want to do to change your life, and not just because you want to marry somebody."

When people come and say they're ready to convert, my first question usually is, "Have you any questions or have you any doubts? Because I don't want you coming into Islam and then realising that you've actually got doubts." One of the women asked, "Do I have to wear a shalwar kameez? Do I have to wear my dupatta?" and I said, "No! You don't! What you come to Islam with is your inner belief. After that, there's going to be times when it's going to be very tough for you. Just take your time. Don't feel that you have to go in head first." Also with clothing, the issue is that it's modest clothing, so whether it's a full length loose skirt with a loose top, that's fine. Yes, it is there that you have to cover your beauty. Your hair is part of your body, it has to be covered. But for a new Muslim, I say to them, "Going from not covering at all, if I'm going to say, 'wrap yourself up', it's too much sometimes." For some it will come naturally and they will just accept everything that's given to them. So I say to them, "Take it one step at a time. At the moment you're not covering at all. You know this is a legal requirement … so give it a day or two. Practice with the scarf, have it around your neck and let it feel a part of your garment. So insha'Allah by the time you do come to wearing the hijab, there won't come a point where you'll feel suffocated. Start slow, keep it steady and lead it to perfection. It's not a one-day thing. It's for your entire life."

Sometimes my number has just been passed along to people I've never met and they've never seen me. They just know me by name and the advantage for them is they don't know me at all. I'm not a Pakistani, I don't speak Punjabi fluently at all, I've got nothing to do with their family, I have no idea about their background and there is no way that they will ever cross my path. Yet I'm a voice on the other end that can hear them out and insha'Allah I can advise them the right way. It gives them that security and added confidentiality. I have wanted to go into counselling, but I see that as a disadvantage because the people that I have managed to serve so far, when it comes to a name, they won't approach it. I'm just a voice without a name so they actually feel very secure. I think that's very important to a lot of women that I've actually helped.

SHAHANA RAHMAN
SALAAM NAMASTE

You must not lose faith in humanity. Humanity is an ocean; if a few drops of the
ocean are dirty, the ocean does not become dirty. (Mohandis Gandhi)

OUR STORIES, OUR LIVES
SHAHANA RAHMAN

I'm Gujarati, married to a Bangladeshi, we run a business with Pakistani friends, my children are British born, so I always say I'm an all-in-one! My parents were Hindu and they were religious, always. My dad used to read the Gita in the morning and he wouldn't have his cup of tea without doing his prayers. I was nearly 18 and I had just completed my teacher training and I had a job interview. My dad's older brother called on my dad and told him about a proposal that he had in mind for me, and they fixed everything up between them. My father loved me a lot, just like a son, and he wanted me to stay in India but my uncle convinced him I would have a better life in England. So my father came home and showed me a picture of my fiancé. I cried and cried because I wanted to stay in India. I loved my father a lot you see. But my dad said, "My older brother is like my father. He has arranged this marriage and I respect his decision. You have to go!" We had a little engagement ceremony in India while the boy was still in England, and then my family put me, all by myself, on a plane to England.

In those days, I'm talking about the 1960s and 1970s, divorce was taboo. It still is and divorcees can suffer a lot of discrimination, people are quick to blame the woman. My marriage was fraught with many challenges. I don't want to go into everything but in my heart I knew that I had tried my best with my marriage, that my uncle had arranged – and now it was time for me to let go. I don't believe that God ever wants to see his creation suffering. I didn't take the decision lightly. My divorce would have made it difficult for my siblings to marry. It would have been deeply disrespectful – unthinkable – for me to broach this topic with my oldest uncle because he was the one who arranged this match. But I didn't know the state of my marriage was old news until I got a letter that my three uncles jointly wrote. It said, "We know how unhappy you are. Don't worry. We understand you can't live with him so you get a divorce." That letter was a rock of support for me during a very difficult period in my life. You know the film *Mother India* – if you don't then you have to watch it, it's an old film. Well, the main character has children to support, she loses her home, her husband loves her but leaves her because he suffers the shame of not being able to support her because he comes to have a disability and he sees himself as a burden. She is treated badly by the corrupt land owner. But still that woman she manages to work hard and build a life for herself. She does not take anything from anyone. Well that is the type of courage I'm talking about.

My son was only one year and nine months when I separated from his father. I was a single parent, a single woman with very few possessions or money. Nowadays it's more acceptable for women to be single and to be doing and going everywhere and more and more are getting married later and later, half the time its difficult for them to find suitable partners so it's a very big problem in our community. But in those days people talked so much. I was all set to return to India for good when I met my second husband at a Bangladeshi friend's house. He was here as a student. After a while my friend suggested we should marry. She knew I needed someone's support, and my son needed a father figure. My second husband took a real shine to my son, and he told me he was committed to giving him a good education. He said we could only marry if both our families accepted the match. His family weren't happy. They didn't understand why a single man wanted to marry a woman with a child. They said, "Does he think he wouldn't be able to get a Bangladeshi girl? There are lots of eligible girls here." So you see there were a lot of judgements if you were a single parent. Why would anyone want to marry a single parent? Yet a man who supports a woman with a child is a very special person, it shows the extent of his love and compassion, doesn't it. Also I was Hindu and he was Muslim so that gave people more to talk about.

I wanted to consult my family elders while I was in India. My father had died and I had an older uncle, the uncle who sent me here. I was so scared. When I tried to talk I felt sick – we respected him that much. I was very surprised by what he said, "… Don't bother about what people say. I would like you to remarry. You can't spend the rest of your life alone." I couldn't believe it. I'm glad he said that. That's why I'm saying I'm a really lucky person because some people wouldn't even want to talk to you, isn't it, when you become a Muslim. For them to allow me to do that at a time when it was such a taboo was a huge thing. And it is always difficult for a divorced woman to remarry especially if she has a child.

My sister couldn't understand how it was possible for a Hindu to become a Muslim. To be honest, I wasn't sure myself to begin with. You know when you change beliefs or religion what is it called, not convert. Yes, apostasy – when you leave one faith – it is considered to be a bad thing and there has been a lot in the news about this, but it says in Quran that 'there is no compulsion in religion'. I think people should not be abused or killed if they choose a different way and I have heard some Sheikhs on TV say this as well. In 1979 I became Muslim. That time it was very hard because Hindu girls that want to become Muslim, nobody liked it. My son was three then and I made him a Muslim a short while after. The imam of the local mosque got me an English book on Islam and its rules and obligations. My friends taught me the namaz, ablutions. My friend and her husband taught me a lot about Islam. Actually, my friend's husband was always going on about the merits of reciting the kalima – how it would take my mind off my worries. He's the one that used to tell me all about Islam and he's the one that inspired me to accept Islam. Well actually, Muslims were very proud. They said I have done a good thing to convert, so they were good to me. But nobody in my community would speak to me; people didn't want to stay in touch. I suppose if a Muslim was to convert to other faith they would probably go through the same thing and rejection. People stopped coming round. Some would say, "You'll see! He'll leave you!" You can't stop tongues wagging, can you! I just thought, 'It's my life. As long as I'm happy with my husband, I don't care what people say!'

But when you choose a different way, which is what I did, then you have to endure the consequence and learn so many different things. I used to do my Hindu prayers and what have you, but I always thought there was only one God. I was worried how I would understand everything – everything is opposite, isn't it. I was used to praying the Hindu way and lighting a diya, while Muslims read the namaz on a prayer mat. But I was keen to learn. I knew some things about Islam already. The main thing was learning the Quran. I still don't know Arabic and I read the Quran in Gujarati. Their way of praying was different but other values were similar, like looking after your parents. One thing I didn't like about Muslims was their tendency to marry their cousins. We didn't do that you see. We thought this was sinful. We tie a rakhi on the wrist of our cousins and call them brother, so they become brothers and unmarriageable to us. I didn't like the idea of men having four wives either, but my husband explained that had been decreed in the olden days as a way to protect women. So I changed my religion, and got married. Then my husband chose a Muslim name for me, Shahana. I was Nirmala before and the funny thing is most of my family still call me Niru. But my colleagues at work started calling me Shahana straight away. They said, "It's a posh name, Shahana. We like it! We'll call you by your new name now!"

I had to change some of my habits. My husband taught me to say 'salaam o alaikum' and 'khuda hafiz'. I was used to saying 'namaste' or 'jayshree krishna'. I used to wear jeans and tops, although I wore saris as well. I negotiated with him and said I wanted to continue wearing bindis on my forehead because I really liked wearing them. He said all right. He also knew how badly I wanted a mangal sutra so he got me one. In India, mangal sutra symbolises your married status. Every married woman wears this special necklace which is always made of gold and black or silver beads. It's a Hindu thing, and as long as your husband is alive, you keep that on, that's all. Nowadays nobody wears it but at that time, it was important. I had been taught to wear it upon marriage, just the way I'd been taught to always wear gold bangles on my wrists when I had a husband. To me, wearing my mangal sutra meant my husband was with me.

I learnt Bengali. It took me about a year. It was quite similar to Gujarati actually. I bought a book and went through it, and whenever I went to a Bengali gathering or a party, we would sit around eating great food and I would sit and listen carefully to the language. All my life, just like most Gujarati Hindus, I had been completely vegetarian. My mum and grandmother had always taught me that eating meat and fish was a sin. I used to cry at first when he'd sit down with his piece of chicken at dinner time. I couldn't bear the smell of it to begin with. My family members couldn't bear the sight and smell of raw meat. I found that so awkward. Then I tried a little piece but I still couldn't bring myself to cook it. I wasn't used to handling it. I would think, 'How am I going to overcome this?' But I eat everything now. I've just got used to it. Even though I'm a Muslim I can't eat beef. I can't even put a morsel of beef in my mouth. Since I was a child, I was taught that the cow is like a mother figure and you worship it, you drink its milk – you don't slaughter it! There were some Muslims in my village in Gujarat and there was a mosque as well. We were all friendly. They ate our food because they knew we didn't cook chicken and things. And when we went to their weddings, they hired a separate cook for the Hindu Gujaratis. But now if you become Muslim you don't have to eat meat, you can be vegetarian, in those days people used to say this and that.

When my mum came to visit me in 1984, many people came to see her, and so things got better after that. People saw my husband was a good man, happy to talk to everyone so then people's attitudes changed. They just wanted to see me happy now. When my mum comes, she makes a little temple in her bedroom so she can pray. It's not like I don't go into that room because I'm not a Hindu anymore. It doesn't matter. In Islam, they say paradise is at the feet of a mother. I do believe that a role of a mother in society is very important, especially now with so much knife and gang crime that is killing so many of our young people. Young people are our future and those of us in a position to help and support them have to do that. When I look back on my life and think about everything that I have been through – it makes me feel proud of everything that I have achieved. It doesn't make any difference to me. I respect all religions. The way I see it, whether you're Muslim, Hindu or Christian, what difference does it make really? We're all God's people! We're all human beings!

ZOHRA J RASHID
The Visionary

Eventually things will have to get better. However the way they will get better is not going to be because of governments, or the elite leadership, or the political leadership, or the institutions of our country.... It will be the people of the country themselves who will bring about the change in society because they have had to struggle to fend for themselves at every level. (Asma Jahangir)

The fire came from our father and went through all of us. We are all reformers in a way. My big sister who was the first headmistress in Rawalpindi region in Pakistan, she must have given at least 30,000 educated women to the region. When my second sister was married, she left her job because her husband said, "You are not working." But my father brought her back! He said, "No! She will work! These are educated women and we need them! They have to work for the nation!" So she came back and she ran another women's school and she must have given about 50,000 educated women to the nation.

The fire within me came from my father. My father was a pioneer of women's education in our region in Pakistan. He was a health supervisor in the district health office. He thought, let's change our women. Let's give her back her brain to think, to work, and to change the destiny of the nation. That's why he sent his daughters away from his house to be educated, and he said, "I am very confident that you will use your education for the betterment of your own family and your own people." There was no provision for learning English when I was a child. My father used to get hold of ex-army men – veterans from World War I and II and they learnt English using their Urdu script, so they would write the English words in Urdu. They learnt the English alphabet but they didn't go further, so they couldn't write a lot and they couldn't speak a lot. They taught me and my big sister many wrong pronunciations.

It was a huge change for me to go from a little town to a university town. I stayed in a women's hostel. It was a prestigious university in Lahore and the atmosphere was really like an international university because at that time, people from all over South Asia started coming to Pakistan. There was a big American influence on the university and that's when I came across *Newsweek* and *The Times* and *Reader's Digest*. In the student union there was not much representation of women so we fought to have two or three seats in the executive body of the union.

I worked as a journalist for a few years and then my father said, "Start a school in this house. We have got five or six rooms. What we need them for? A head teacher, she is a general. She directs an army of people you see, so you will be your own king here. The nation needs educated people and give them moral grooming also, you know, being nice human beings." This was 1967. I won't say it was an investment because it was not. The rate of my charges was so nominal I didn't earn anything for three years. And I had to buy blackboards, globes, maps, furniture. For me it was about satisfaction. By that time, you see mentally I was Florence Nightingale. Mentally I was a big health worker and a social worker. I wanted to serve the community around me in my mohalla in Rawalpindi. The people around me were down to earth poor. They didn't have access to a penny worth of aspro or quinine to get rid of malaria or any painkiller to get rid of a headache. They didn't have any thought of being educated or giving education to their children. Most of them had migrated from villages to earn their living in the city, and the city didn't have any means to give them jobs or accommodation so they were living in ghettoes and huts. So in that environment, how could you speak of giving them a good education or good healthcare?! They didn't have anything!

In those circumstances, starting an education centre in the middle of a mohalla where people were looking for these opportunities you see, I think it was prophetic and I did it. In Urdu you say you burnt your blood – I worked hard! In one or two months we had 300 kids, boys and girls. I employed girls, BA pass and FA pass. In six months we had 600 kids. It was a big deal. In Pakistan at that time and still there were just a few government schools and the population was growing. The streets were just full of teenagers and the parents did not have the means to send them to good high standard schools.

I came from a big family. All my sisters were married and they had their own children. By staying in the city I was a headquarter for them. They used to send their children to stay with me to get higher education in colleges and universities, so in that way I was a shelter for everybody. Family members and other people that knew us would come and stay in that house if they were looking for a job. They would say, "Find me a job!" so I was a job centre too. Even if somebody needed a blood transfusion they would come to me and I would arrange it.

I got married when I was 36, but I wanted even later than that! I was not prepared and I was very busy with other things you see. By the time of my marriage I was very successful and I was in a very powerful position. I was! The standard of my school was quite good as compared to others in the area, and the education office knew I was outspoken and I could discuss education. I stood up against Mr Bhutto when the price of milk doubled overnight. One morning we realised it had gone up and many of the parents said it was too much. I gathered the staff and I said, "We have to take a stand. It's our right. We can't afford it." The next morning we took a big demonstration with the older students, my staff, about 40 parents and my friends.

I think by that time my family had accepted that I hadn't shown any inclination towards marriage. Actually my family was quite backward in that way. They didn't marry the daughters out of the family, and there was not a suitable person for me in the family. It was their thinking that nobody is equal to us so that's why they didn't give their daughters out of the family. Two of my cousins who are of my age and highly educated, and still they are unmarried at the age of 65!

We just took pride in being unmarried and living with the family if there is no suitable person, and it was not only pride, no. It was also that we are not going to dishonour our families by marrying on our own. When I started college my father gave me this hint, and at that time I was writing romantic stories and he knew that this is the age that people can get carried away and this and that. One day we were talking about something and he said, "Look, in the end the girls are going to go away to get married, but we can't give a chair to anyone else except from our own family." It means we are not going to accept someone out of the family. And I understood it and kept quiet and I kept these sacred words with me until the last. I was an obedient child. We were brought up to believe we should do whatever brings respect and honour to our family. And marrying on your own or choosing your own spouse or being rebellious, it was considered to be bad at that time. So despite my education, I still maintained that traditional outlook, yes I did.

There were many male colleagues. There were so many things that people liked in me. There were many good suitors and I liked many. But I didn't give a lift to any man that looked towards me. Until my marriage I didn't have a big romance or anything. My reputation was flawless. In the first place when I was in my 20s, I said, "I am not going to do it. No, I am not going to hurt my family." And then after my 30s, I was a successful person and I became choosy. I thought, 'The person should be like me – outstanding, mature, the right person.' And by 36 or 37, there was no person like that. Little choice was left by that stage. My mother was very

worried about me. She said, "You have brought up the families of your sisters and brothers and they are not very supportive. The kids of other people don't look after you. They don't care in what situation are you. It's only your own kids that love you and care for you. You can't get that love from the children of other people. And you can't depend on them and I can't die without marrying you. I will get you married!" And I said, "OK, if you want to get me married, look for a proper person. I am not going to marry the people you are suggesting!"

And then this man came from England, and he was from my family. And I had this image that yes I am going to marry a tall person, a handsome person and a generous person. And luckily he was generous and he was handsome and tall. And luckily he was impressed by my intellect. It takes a secure man to appreciate a woman's intellect and capacity to contribute in dynamic ways. When he went back, he had many rishtas and he gave them grading – 'this girl is beautiful', 'she is homely', but 'this girl is intelligent and bold'. I refused but he said, "No, I am not listening no!" And I thought, 'Oh, he's not listening no! Ok!' I think it was his generosity in the end. He was at heart a reformer like me. He was a better educationist than me and his approach was philosophical all the time. He was a groomed educated person, nice and polite. I liked him then. Yes, he was very critical all the time and that annoyed me, but otherwise he was ok.

He brought me to Bradford in 1977. My husband was not the mixing type and I was staying in the house for hours and hours. I wrote an article in the T&A – 'a lonely person on a little island', something like that, and they published it and afterwards there was no ending! People rang me. People came here to see me – organisations, individuals, women's associations, Mothers' Union – so many people! By the winter of '78, I gave about 13 talks on Pakistani culture, dishes, our beautiful dress and traditions and other things in various mothers' unions, churches and parishes. Then people from Bradford Teaching College, they came and they asked me to talk about peace. I was taken as a very pampered person. It all went very well and I was thrilled.

Racism came in 1980 and '81 when people started spitting at us. It happened to me. Once I was walking up the street and two young men, they were passing the road. They came near us and they just spat on my daughter. Some came on me also. I was taken aback. I was shocked. I said something but they had gone. My daughter cried. She cried. I brought her home and washed her. I was bitter. I thought, 'What's going to happen now? The world is changing,' and I talked to many people and they said they had already experienced things like that. At that time it was not anti-Islamic or terrorism. It was perhaps that people started coming in abundance from the subcontinent and the English people, they felt threatened. They did not want people coming and overtaking them. I think that was the cause of it, too much people coming here and taking over businesses and everything.

In this predominantly Asian area we were not so scared but when we heard about skinhead marches in other areas and one or two times, we also heard they are coming this way, we were scared and we thought we should shut ourselves in and not be seen. Those were bad times. We were scared and I kept my children in and other people also did the same. But that was a short phase I think. It was quickly changed because many government initiatives started talking about harmony and racial mixing and everything. The work had started by that time and it was coming on the media, but yes the fear was there. I think until '84 it was a lot still there because some Asian youth were trying to organise in groups to face skinheads or National Front, now you have the BNP – they're very clever and try to divide communities with their bad politics.

The riots in Bradford were sad times and I think people in other parts of England got a bad impression of the Muslim community. I felt sorry for the mothers of the boys who ended up in prison as well. It is difficult for a mother! You see most people were expecting that something will happen because the tension between the police and Asian youth was there. People were talking about the changing attitudes in Asian youth and more racism on the part of police. It was general ethos that whenever our youth go to the police station they are not treated fairly. There were a few voices on the political side who were asking people to leave the country and this and that, so the atmosphere on the whole was not very conjugal. People were feeling it's not going the right way. Young Asian boys they were adamant to face this situation and even before that evening, there was some show of power from Asian youth in that area. How the riots started I think two or three people were arrested and they were not treated nicely in the police station.

OUR STORIES, OUR LIVES
ZOHRA J RASHID

And when Isabelle rang me, she said, "The boys are gathering and the parents are very worried around the police station on Oak Lane, and we should do something about it. We should go there with a white flag of peace because we are a peace group."

It was summer, six or seven in the evening, and I grabbed my car keys and ran outside. My husband ran outside after me and he said, "No, you are not going. There will be fights. Those young men are going to do something and you women you can't stop them. Don't go." I felt helpless – very annoyed and very angry. I didn't know what to do. I think it was my weakness. Despite my being so courageous in many ways, I never denied anything to my husband. I tried not to infuriate him. It was not the consequences that there will be a fight – nothing like that. I just thought I shouldn't annoy him – but he also cared and I could see in his eyes that he didn't want me to be hurt. I don't know what it was. I submitted most of the time, but this was the time not to submit. It was for a good cause. And I felt very bad not joining forces with my amazing friends on that night.

The boys were in quite good strength – 60 or 70 boys – and they were ready to fight. They were ready to die there! And they were very tense, and people around the area were very worried. And these women, my friends, they walked with candles and the white flag of peace and one of them had written underneath in Urdu 'Aman, Aman, Aman' which means peace. And when they walked in, they were very daring and very courageous. They achieved a lot. The boys looked at them and they saw that there were also some Pakistani ladies with chaddar on, and they looked at their faces. They felt some motherly figures, sisterly figures, they had come to rescue them from a calamity. The police got relaxed. At last there was a neutral force to stop all this. That changed attitude in Bradford, I think that is a result of that daring thing which the women did.

I felt very bitter about not being a part of it. I felt I was the right person to go there and play a part in it. I wanted to work for peace and friendship and this was an opportunity to be part of it. It was a great thing and I missed it. But I am very very happy about my friends who did this and I am always full of praise and I salute them.

Zehida Rehman
Turning Pennies into Pounds

*A friend is one to whom one can pour out all the contents of ones heart,
chaff and grain together, knowing that the gentleness of hands will take and sift
it, keeping what is worth keeping, and, with the breath of kindness, blow the
rest away. (Arabic proverb)*

In my younger days – I'm 36 now – my parents had a shop and I used to help out. You know those jars of sweets that they used to sell in quarters in them days? Well, I took two bags, two quarters to school one day. They cost me maybe 20p and I had these big toffee sweets you see and I sold them for 10p each so I must have made about 60p on one of those bags of sweets. That's where I got interested in making money. I must only have been about 12 then. It was good having some money and giving some to your brothers and sisters and going, "Here buy yourselves something." And I remember my sister did Avon and she used to have sample perfumes and those little lipsticks. I used to take them to school and my English friends go, "Can we buy some?" My sister used to get them for about 10p and there were six in a pack, and I sold each one for 5p. So it just seemed good having money and making money like that. It was from these very humble beginnings that I became interested in business, I learnt very quickly about what people liked and didn't like. My brother had a clothes shop and he used to go to Manchester, and one day I asked, "Can I go along with you?" I bought some little dress rings. You get a pack of them for about £3 and there were 12 in them. I took them to school and sold them for about 50p each. Then my brother put a market stall and I asked, "Can I buy some toys and sell them there?" I must have been about 15 then. So from sweets, to Avon perfumes, to stalls I've done a lot of different things and through all of this slowly but surely I was building my confidence. I'd always dreamt of being my own boss and now I am. I like working for myself because nobody's telling you what to do. All it takes is a little bit of enthusiasm, a bit of ambition and a lot of hard work. I'm a doer and not a watcher!

When I was running my own takeaway restaurant I used to go to the cash and carry, all the guys and even the workers used to stare at me because it was so strange for a woman to go in and buy something. I still get it today. They say things like, "Why do you work for? You don't need to work! A husband should work, not a woman! My wife is at home looking after her babies, and so should you!" That's what the guys say. I take the remarks with a pinch of salt really, there's always that bit of chauvinism and jealousy. You learn to laugh it off. They wouldn't say things like that to people like Perveen Warsi – the Asian millionaire woman who started her business with nothing and made it huge and the Prophet's first wife Khadeja who was a talented business woman in her own right. I don't want nobody including my husband saying, "I provided for you!" I feel proud that I'm working and whatever I've done, I've done it myself.

My other venture started when I used to take my daughters to the new school for girls in West Bowling. One of the girl's parents approached me and asked me to collect their child and she offered to pay me. Someone else asked after a few weeks and then another and another. There was a clear demand and I saw it as a real opportunity to help others. So I did my bit of simple research and got something done. Sometimes people think you have to do huge reports, me I'm simple. I'm sure there are lots of women who want to set up their own business but the bureaucracy puts them off. Too many people sit back and watch but sometimes you have to take risks even if it means failing at first you just have to get up and brush the dust off, move on and try something else! I asked the school if they were thinking about getting a minibus but they weren't. So I asked them to write a letter to all the parents asking if it would be worthwhile for me to get a minibus. I got a good response and so a couple of us got together and got a minibus. You see they prefer a woman driver. Most of the girls, their dad's either a taxi driver or he's working nights so he can't drop them off in the morning, or they've got a few other kids that have to be dropped off, and some of the mums don't drive.

So this was the perfect solution. I take 16 girls to school every day now and drop them off as well. Before I pick up each girl, I give them a miss call from my mobile to her house which gives her about three minutes to come out. Like if I'm late by 10 minutes, that's them waiting outside on the main road. So I make sure I'm always punctual. A lot of the girls wanted me to stop at the shop during the school run because they wanted to buy chocolates and crisps at home time, so they'd be like, "Auntie," – that's what they call me, everyone is either an auntie or an uncle – "please will you stop so I can get a drink?" I did that a few times. I thought, 'Why don't I get the sweets and sell them to the girls myself.' I buy them and put them all in a big see through box – you know sweets, drinks, crisps, chocolate. My first customers were the girls that went to school with me in the minibus, but then as soon as the other girls in the school found out, they all started coming out. So I'd be in the car park and the bell would go for home time, and next thing I knew everybody would be stood there near my van buying crisps and chocolate and that. I used to make like 10p on each bar so it worked out cheaper for the girls to buy off me and at the end of the day, I was making a little money on it as well.

When I started doing that, my husband used to say, "Forget it! What do you do that for?" But while I'm sat there I'm probably making like a £1 or £2. That's where it starts you know, you have to show respect to the pennies and they'll turn into pounds. And at the end of the day, that change that I make I can spend on my kids.

I have a big family, when I had my son, he'd be taken to see his step sisters and they thought he was really cute. But one day he bumped his head and they phoned me. That's how I got talking to Shafina, my husband's first wife. She says she's going to stay here with her mother-in-law because our mother-in-law is related to her as well. She doesn't want to go back to Pakistan. The fact that she's got two daughters as well, and they were my husband's daughters, it just wouldn't have been fair on them to have to go to Pakistan. They were born here. I've been to Pakistan myself. It's a man's world over there. The country's so beautiful but it's poor and you can't do anything and most women don't work and culturally you have to rely on a man. The government doesn't have a proper welfare system, like income support and other benefits you get here. Maybe at first she was jealous and I was, but as time goes on, you accept so many things. And at the end of the day, I just thought if she's ok with me and she's ok with my kids, then I've got nowt to lose, and she says the same. We've become friends. She used to call me over and make some food for me and she'd look after my son because I was working. Then her girls needed to buy some school uniforms and I ended up taking them. She knows how I am and I know what she's like. We're the same age. We've got three girls and two boys between us. If someone asks how many kids I've got, I just say five and so does she. It's something that feels very natural to say now because all of us have become so close.

In the morning I do the school run so Shafina gets the kids ready and in the holidays I do it. She looks after the housework and I look after everything outside because she doesn't know a lot of English. She can't drive but I'm teaching her because I want her to feel a bit more independent so that she can do something for herself. When our mother-in-law was in Pakistan recently, I took Shafina and the girls to a few restaurants and took them shopping. It's about showing her there's life outside home as well. Now she helps out in my café. She wouldn't do it before but I say, "You have to!" I say, "If you're not going to learn, later on anything could happen. Social are not going to let you stay at home. You'll have to work. It's different now!" This way, she's meeting people, she's gaining confidence in her English and she's handling money and sorting out prices. This way, she's supporting herself now. If I have an argument with my mother-in-law, she sticks up for me. You know what mother-in-laws can be like, but Shafina will stand by me. And if we need to go to somebody's house she'll go with me. Sometimes if I'm not home and it's getting late, she'll ring me to say, "Your food's getting cold. Aren't you coming going to have something to eat?" And it feels nice that somebody's waiting and cares.

For some people they would find it difficult to understand the relationship we have – how two women can learn to work together and overcome the awkwardness but at the end of the day, if we weren't happy, this just wouldn't have worked.

Shafina's compromised. I've compromised and that's how it's worked out. If I was by myself now with my kids and without Shafina, it's not that I wouldn't cope. It's just then I would close the café earlier when the kids finish school and probably give more responsibility to my husband. And I probably wouldn't run two businesses, like the minibus and the café – probably just one. Her daughters are teenagers now and she usually appreciates me talking to them about stuff, growing up you know all of that stuff. I think I can explain things in English far better than she can. In lots of ways we're complete opposites, I was brought up here she was born and brought up in Pakistan. She loves going to weddings and I hate going. I don't like the fact that you have to dress up, wear your make-up, wear your jewellery, just to show people what you've got, and they wear stuff that's 10 times flashy than you. It's a competition! And I'm a simple person who'll just wear what's convenient for me and that's it. I am most comfortable in jog pants and a T-shirt. Shafina loves dressing up and all that. She wears like flashy dupattas, shalwar kameez, make-up, high heels, puts her hair up in a plait or with clips and stuff. She wears her gold bangles, rings and her other bracelets and her necklace set and all that. Weddings are a big deal for her because there she meets everyone from Pakistan, like people she grew up with and I understand that. She looks forward to going. When she gets a wedding invitation, she'll tell me the same day and I'm like, "Oh God, all right, I'll go!" She's compromised so much for me so I go to the weddings even though I don't like them. Although when she does go, she drags about three people with her so I have to take all of them then! With men, they say they come from a different world, don't they! Women think differently. With Shafina I can tell her anything, ask her to do anything and she'll just get on with it. I depend on her now. I rely more on Shafina than I do on my husband. Shafina knows what I'm like. She knows I don't laze about. I work and I pay all the bills jointly with my husband. Shafina gives me respect and she gets it back. As the new generations grow older – the traditional ways of doing things are changing.

In my family it was dad that worked and my mum used to stay at home and look after the kids. You know at that time, my grandparents wouldn't let me go to college because they would say, "In our family nobody goes to college out of the girls." It was the way they were, their upbringing so when we did do things they were considered big and bold steps in our family. If we did anything that was thought to be too much, then everybody got involved and there were discussions and debates. A woman she makes the house comfortable for the family and looks after the kids and saves money as well. I believe that without a woman, a guy can't go forward. And the thing is the guy goes out and works and he comes home thinking he's done more work than the woman, and I don't believe that…! My experiences have shaped the way my husband and me choose to bring my daughters up now. They're watching and learning from me and the way I run my businesses as well as bringing them up. I want them to be independent and intelligent young women who know what they want from life and who don't have to depend on anyone!

ULFAT RIAZ
BUSING IN THE IMMIGRANTS

Even after all this time, the sun never says to the earth "You owe me". Look what happens with a love like that. It lights the whole sky. (Hafiz of Persia)

I was born in Pakistan. We lived between Rawalpindi and Jhelum in a village called Morgah, which growing up everyone says, "chicken town, chicken town, chicken village", and then I find out Morgah means peacock town! I came to England when I was three. But to be honest most of my family's still back in Pakistan. I've got two older sisters that are married there. They've got their kids and grandkids there. I've got my aunts, my uncles, my in-laws, my first cousins, my second cousins removed – the whole shenanigans are back in Pakistan! So there's only a few members of my family here. I mean, here I've got my mum, dad, four sisters, one brother. Then I've got me, my husband, one of my sister-in-laws, her children, my husband's uncle, his children. So I would say there's about 10 or 15 houses that belong to our family from back home that live here, not even that many actually.

I think that's quite unusual for us in that we didn't bring everybody across, like some of the communities. With some of the other communities I can understand with the level of poverty and situation they existed in, like if you look at the Mirpur community, you had the whole Mangla Dam episode. You had displacement of people, whole villages, and so people had to go somewhere, and you know Britain was the ideal opportunity and that's what happened. In our village, my grandparents were educated. My dad's dad was a sergeant in the army and he used to write letters to me in English as I was growing up. My father-in-law used to write letters for everybody and stuff so the men folk in our village were educated. They were poor, no doubt about it. They were poor in the way that my father did come out of Pakistan looking to support his family. Poverty was common among Pakistanis that came in the early days. Even now you see it, I think Asians especially Pakistanis and Bangladeshis live in some of the poorest areas in the country right now. You see I was born in 1963 and I think my dad got his visa to leave the country just before I was born so they always see me as an omen of good faith. I don't bloody think so! If this is an omen of good faith, then they've lost the plot somewhere along the line! Then me and my mum came over in 1965, straight to Bradford.

I lived in a place called Hanover Square, which was the most beautiful place on planet earth as far as I was concerned, because we lived in a square shaped street, and in the middle we had a massive, massive park with dense trees, which we called the jungle! And through all my childhood, that was our heaven. It was our place where we all used to play all the time. And you know what the community was like? Well, they were all Pathans except for our house and my auntie's house. So I had a load of girlfriends but when they were 10 or 11, they stopped playing out – something to do with coming of age or maturity. So I used to start playing with their brothers instead! All my life my best friends have always been boys – not in a bad way, but you play with whoever's out there, don't you, when you're a kid.

I went to a school on the outskirts of Bradford called Bolton Woods. That was about three miles from where we lived, and because where we lived it was predominantly Asian, so I didn't go to the schools around there. I used to stand on the corner of my street which was the pick-up point, and the bus would come and maybe pick up 80 or 90 kids – all Asian kids – and then on its way it would drop one batch off at Frizinghall School, which was a predominantly white school, and then the rest of us at Bolton Woods School. So most of the kids in that school were white except for us few scattered brownie points for the government!

At that time it was the government's policy to bus kids out into white areas, for integration purposes you know. The teachers used to call us the immigrants. When it was home time, they used to say, "Will the immigrants please stand on one side and wait for your bus," and that's how we were addressed. Because we were thrown from a great height into an all white school, you had no choice but to learn. But I don't think kids can integrate. Children are children, you have to understand that! Regardless of what colour they are, they are children, and they will play with a person not because of their colour but because they get on with that person. So you're best friends with Tracey and Julie and June, right, but you're not best friends with Yasmin, and that wasn't because some were white and more superior and the Asians were less so, that had nothing to do with it. You were best mates with Tracey and Julie because they were your best mates! People should just leave childhood alone and they should just let kids get on with the game of growing up and understanding.

I mean, they didn't know any better than me, and we used to walk around singing, "All join on with no Pakis on." What was a Paki? I didn't know what a Paki was until I was 13 or the significance of what that meant. And you know, we'd all walk arm in arm and all the kids would join in and chant this. And all the Asian kids would be chanting with you arm in arm. And then you'd sing, "All join on with no whities on" and you had white kids singing with you as well. I've just been hearing about Prince Harry and how he used the word Paki, to refer to his "little Paki friend". To be honest with you we need to look at the racism within our own community towards people of other backgrounds, colours, faiths too. But you know what – people have a tendency to make mountains out of molehills they really do. There is far too much political correctness about! Leave the poor guy alone! For me it's what goes in front and behind of that term that really matters. If it was someone like Nick Griffin, head of the BNP, saying it then it's an issue. Even people like him you learn to ignore. I don't for one minute believe that there was any malice intended when Prince Harry said it. People need to lighten up a little, we take everything so seriously nowadays. We need to learn to laugh at ourselves more, for heaven's sake lighten up!

Back then, they knew we didn't eat pork or we didn't eat meat. So we had the same menu but they made allowances for the immigrant kids by not dishing up the meat for us. So we always had fish and vegetarian, and we were deprived of sausages and meat and potato pie, steak and kidney pie. We used to watch the English kids eat their gravy and mash and think, 'Oh God! What I wouldn't do to have some of that!' but we never had it because it wasn't halal. And I went to that school till I was nine or 10. My upper school was the worst school ever. It was an all girls' school which is the worst thing any parent can do is send their child to a single-sex school. It was horrible because I grew up with loads of lads and I was very much of a tomboyish character. And the girls at school were into make-up, hair and all that kind of stuff, and we just never did it at our house. For me it just wasn't there. So school did nothing for me, absolutely nothing. The day I left school, I kissed the ground and thanked God that I would never have to return to that goddamned place again! And I never have been back.

I was never into the boyfriend stuff either. I wasn't going out with anybody. Like most of my friends always had a boyfriend and they were always crying and moaning about stuff, "He's done this! He's done that!" I never had any of that. I just wasn't interested. I was more into my books and music I was such a fan of Pink Floyd, Mo Town you know Stevie Wonder, Diana Ross, Roy Oberson, The Beatles. In the '80s it was Wham, Duran Duran, Bananarama not to mention all the Qwaalis I went through. You name it and I knew it. And then one day my parents said, "Right you're getting married now and this is the person you're going to marry. This is the guy we've chosen." So I say, "fine". You just didn't bother. You just didn't ask questions. You just did it. Well, I mean we did debate about it like I say, "Dad, do you know what you're doing?" and all the rest of it. But I accepted it. So I got married when I was about 20. Nowadays marriage contracts are all the rage but back then you didn't even know what one of those was. It was hectic actually, everything happened so quickly. And the wedding bloody went on for days and the drums were as loud as ever! And my mum and dad had this massive fuck off wedding which drove me absolutely mental and it was just my mum and dad's thing, wasn't it! It was just like, "What the fuck! Why are you wasting so much money on a wedding – doing all this? You don't need to do this!" Well, they did it and I got married!

My mum took me to Bombay Stores and bought me like 20 suits, and I had the best bari in the whole of Bradford for like 10 years. Nowadays people down South have an image of Northerners, they call Bradford Bradistan! Or it's that "that backward place". You'll always get the usual North–South politics, it's funny sometimes because it's the cockneys or toffs versus the Eeee by gums and don't mention the Brummies! But in those days people came up North because you couldn't get many things elsewhere especially spices and clothes and all that, we were the equivalent of China Town in Manchester or London. Anyway my mum was really fashionable, you know in her clothes sense. So she knew what she was buying and she bought me such beautiful clothes. You see I was never prim and proper. I didn't even wear shalwar kameez till I was about 15, and my cousins had all these fancy shalwar kameez all the time. And we had hand-me-downs and stuff from other cousins. So it was like the first time ever my mum got me all these clothes, I mean beautiful stuff. I mean that was about as exciting as it got, I think.

On my wedding night, I sat there and my husband came in and sat next to me. And he started talking. God knows what he was saying. I wasn't listening. My head was buzzing because I was so tired. He offered me a fag and I took it. And we sat there, on the back of the bed, knees up, ashtray between us and a packet of fags. It was like, "What the hell's gone on! Bloody hell! Wasn't that a crazy day!" And that's the conversation I was having with my husband on the first night!

We've had three children now. My husband has always been an incredible support to me. I think he's the only one that puts up with me and my outrageous zest for life. He talks to the kids about identity. He says the most important thing is your identity; who you are, your faith, your culture. He goes, "As long as you're steady in your faith, you'll never lose sight of who you are." My husband prays and yet he never enforced it on his children. We would fast and we would do things as a family together, but forcing the issue was never our way of doing things. And I think that's the beauty about him and that's what kept us together and kept our family close. My son's been reading namaz for a very long time. He's really into his faith. And with my daughter, in the middle of university she saw this scholarship at Galilee University. So she goes, "I'm going to do some research into Islam because the last thing I want is for anybody to ask me any questions about my faith. I want to be able to answer it." So she started researching and researching, and researching.

So one day, I went to pick up my daughter from her friend's house and she came out and she had the hijab on. Whatever was going on for her, me and my husband didn't know, but her brother and her sister knew. Then I found out a friend she used to hang around with who wore a baseball cap a lot was also a hijabi, but because she couldn't wear a hijab all the time, she'd wear a baseball cap instead to hide her hair. So my daughter got in the car and I say to her, "So, is this the way you're thinking of going?" And she says, "Yes! I've been practising at home. I went to an Islamic meeting today and that's the first time that I wore it out. But I don't know if I'm ready to wear it in Bradford and at uni and stuff." So we went home and I was still quite gobsmacked to be honest. And she was testing out the hijabs she'd bought with all her outfits. Then the next day she came in to my work and she had a green hijab on and she goes, "I'm off to uni and I've decided to wear it."

For her it was spiritual enlightenment. And we were very happy for her, and I don't want to use the word 'proud' because that's saying we weren't proud of her anyway. But we were humbled because I think we are blessed to have children in our life that are able to find the right path, at such a young age, out of their own free will and choice. I don't think I've got it.

I mean, the way I see it, I have my own relationship with God. I do my namaz. I do my Quran. I do it when I want to do it and when God needs me to do it, I will do it. It has nothing to do with anybody else, and that is what faith is about. We are at the end of the day responsible for our own actions. I love the wind in my hair! If people ask me, I say there is nothing more beautiful than having my hair open and feeling the wind in my hair and I don't want to give that up for anything. God hasn't asked me yet, and when he does, I will do!

AKHTAR SHEIKH
WHITE ABBEY ROAD

And so our mothers and grandmothers have, more often than not anonymously, handed on the creative spark, the seed of the flower they themselves never hoped to see or like a sealed letter they could not plainly read.... (Alice Walker)

W e Sheikhs are naturally business-minded people. All my brothers were businessmen. I'd watched them bring home sackfulls of money and I was their sister. I knew me and my husband had to work hard if we were going to make something of ourselves in England, and I was ready. I had the grandest shop on White Abbey Road!

We had a house in Weston Street just off White Abbey Road. No Pakistanis then, just us! My husband was a manager in a factory, working on the looms. You know I'd come from this big tight-knit family and I was all alone when I got to England. I only had two children then. One day a friend took me to a Hindu woman on Leeds Road, Kohli we called her, to get some fabric. This Hindu woman had rolls of fabric laid out on a bed and she was selling it. And she was really sweet tongued she was, persuasive you know. I noted each and every detail about her. I thought, 'What a clever woman! She's selling dupattas worth 10 or 20 shillings to our Mirpuri women for a pound apiece.' I knew my prices you know, and I had a really good head for maths, so I came home and did a few sums.

I said to my husband, "Please get me some fabric like she's got so I can sell it too. If that Kohli woman can do it, I definitely can." And he goes, "Have you gone mad? Got some money, have you?" And I told him, "Yes! I've got a thousand pounds in the bank actually!" I'd been drawing the family allowance and putting it straight in the bank, and getting by on whatever my husband brought home. He earned about £17 back then. And I told my husband there's eight or 10 Pakistani women that come to drop off their kids at our son's school. I'll write them all a note with my address and my son will give them out to the aunties at school. I told him to invite the women home and tell them my mum's got fabric for sale at home. I convinced my husband.

So we got some fabric from the Jewish wholesalers in Manchester. I gathered the most beautiful fabrics, chiffons and prints. And my husband was stunned that first Saturday because so many people turned up to our house. You see, you couldn't get the sort of fabric us women wanted to wear back then. English people sold fabric but it was really thick stuff. My stuff was so popular. It's all about choice you know and I had such

good taste. We sold out in a week and we had to go back to Manchester to get more.

I bumped into another woman, Pushba, at the clinic where I took the children. It turned out she was also stocking fabric in her house. She lived in the same neighbourhood. She didn't know I was doing the same thing so she said, "Akhtar, you must come to my house. I've got fabric!" I put my kids in the pram and off I went looking for her house. Do you know, she was even more clever than me. She was really pretty as well, slim and fair skinned, all dressed up in a sari. I really wanted to know who was supplying her with Japanese fabrics but she wouldn't give anything away.

I kept going to Pushba's to see what she was up to and she opened up her shop on White Abbey Road three months before me. She was really jealous when she saw it was me that was opening up another cloth shop in the area. She goes, "You! But you're Muslim! Muslim women wear bhurkas and they do purdah, and look at you with a shop!" I told her, "Bhurka! I don't wear one, dear! I left mine in Karachi! It's my heart that tells me I'm a Muslim!" Those were honourable times you see, and I just thought, 'What have I got to be ashamed of? My husband's right behind me, and I'm a bold woman.' I knew I'd be all right.

When I opened Sheikh Fabrics in 1963, we had so many customers from London, I can't even tell you. There was no fabric shops in London then, and people used to come to Bradford to buy it. The Mirpuris would come with empty suitcases and they'd only leave once those cases were full. Each one would spend £100. All their shopping from Bradford. I charged a little more but the women still came to me. I'd make them tea sometimes and I tried to be really friendly. They'd say, "Mrs Sheikh's fabrics are very good!" You know the women that were used to wearing the nicer fabrics, those that had a bit of taste, they always bought from me.

I had the shop open from nine in the morning and I was lucky if the customers let me close for the night at 10! My husband was always happy to roll up his sleeves and muck in, whether it was in the shop or in the kitchen, and he'd look after the kids in the evening – feeding and bathing them – while I was busy in the shop. Then he left his job in the factory and worked with me. But if he manned the shop on his own, then the women didn't come in, especially the women from Mirpur. I'd have white people coming into the shop wanting to know what our people did with all that fabric. I'd tell them people take the fabric back to Pakistan, to give to their brothers and sisters. They bought suitcases full so we started selling luggage as well. We'd sell them a suitcase and then they'd buy enough fabric to fill it as well.

We used to make £2,000 profit every week in those days! Can you believe it! This was from 1965 to about 1980, we were really busy with that shop. We had cash stashed underneath the mattresses and no time to get it to the bank. We had to get a safe in the end and even that was always stuffed full. Our women did whisper about me. They'd say, "Mrs Sheikh is the first to be running a fabric store, and she's not embarrassed at all about having to deal with men. Her husband doesn't even stop her. Her head's not covered. She talks to men." I knew I wasn't doing anything wrong, and I had my husband's support but I didn't want to offend my clients. It wasn't worth it so I tried to ensure I always had my head covered – because of these people, to stop the gossip mongers.

You see a man makes his wife feel secure if he supports her. Nobody points the finger if you've got your husband with you, and people are free to gossip if you haven't. That was the norm in our society and we knew that. No matter how useless your man is, no matter how pathetic, he's still a support to you because he's a man. And when a woman supports her man, she helps him to blossom. My father-in-law was really proud of the way I pushed his son and made something of him, and of the way I had raised our six children while working so hard myself.

By the time my husband fell ill, we had three shops in Whetley Lane. We had the Kebabeesh Restaurant, we had Whetley Lane Food Store and I had a shop called Chaman Cloth. But I gave up the fabric shop anyway when my husband fell ill. I could see he was getting weaker. He had cancer. He knew he was dying. He used to say to me, "I'm going to be with God." We'd been together from the time I was 17 to the time I was 50. You have to strengthen your heart when it happens on you. You have to wise up. When he passed away, we were all sitting on the floor and Pushba came to see me. She had become a close friend and when she heard, like everyone else, that Mr Sheikh from White Abbey Road had died, she came just like everyone else did. She held me and whispered in my ear, "This is not the time for you to cry. You need to prepare yourself now. You need to focus. Don't start depending on your children. Get a grip and maintain control of everything. Don't let your children take over now." She gave me good advice and I didn't mind it.

I was alone. That's how it feels when you lose your other half. But at least I had my own money so I didn't need to depend on anyone. I didn't realise how important that was though until my husband had passed away. Being financially independent gave me strength. Even now, it's been 25 or 26 years since I lost my husband, and I don't have to put up with anyone telling me what to do. I can call the shots because I have my own money.

RINA (RADHIA) TARAFDER
THE SPIRITUAL TOURIST

You can write me down in history with hateful, twisted lies, you can tread me in this very dirt, but still, like dust, I'll rise. (Maya Angelou)

OUR STORIES, OUR LIVES
RINA (RADHIA) TARAFDER

I grew up in a Muslim family and I think my exposure to religion was quite wholesome. I wasn't told to just do things because you have to just do them. Things were explained to me, whether it's respect for people, respect for the community, or whether it was prayers or fasting, it was explained to me and more than just, "Well, we've got to do it because we're told we have to; that's what it says." That was from my father, but the community experience of religion put me off Islam. That saying, 'religion is the opium of the masses', really struck a chord. And I went, 'Oh yeah! It is! Can you just see these people? They just don't think outside of what they've been told to believe.' And very early on, I went back home to Bangladesh and I saw these old Buddhist shrines, and I thought, 'We weren't always Muslims. It's only because I was born in a Muslim family that I'm Muslim today.' Spiritually I felt a little bit Buddhist as well and I felt 'Hmmm, maybe I'm Buddhist' in the way that Black Americans go back to Islam. I kind of related to that. But then I thought, 'If I get into this Buddhist thing, that's completely dangerous territory within my community.' Because if I were to convert or say I'm a Buddhist, I couldn't even say that my parents would disown me because I don't know what would happen. I just know it wouldn't be good. So I thought, 'Ok! Before I go any further with this and wreak complete havoc, I need to explore where I'm at and who I am first.'

As a result I then started reading about Islam. I just wanted to explore it. I just felt like, if I'm going to do something else, I need to know and have my arguments ready so that was really my angle. I needed to be clear not just for the community but for myself as well. I didn't want to be a spiritual tourist throughout my life. And I thought, I'll start with Islam, then I'll go to Buddhism, then I'll go to Christianity, and I thought I'd go through the lot. I wasn't very religious, if anything I was very feminist and I was very aware of women and their status and power, and lack of power. And the first book I read on Islam, I was so horrified by it, that I threw it across the room. It was very limiting and it was so against my feminism that I hated it, but it didn't put me off from reading about Islam. Through my reading, I started to find that the version of Islam that was filtering through into my heart and my soul appealed to my feminist side and I took that feeling very, very seriously. I was reading the Quran alongside and started to get to know what was in the Quran. I was getting more and more involved and engaged and stimulated by it. It was fantastic, and I found that Islam just fell into place for me.

As it stands I live with my two sons who are 14 and 12, and it's just me and them. As far as relationships were concerned I always felt that when I got married he has got to be Bengali, he's got to be at least five or six years older than me. He's got to be of a certain educational standard – he's got to be a graduate and he's got to be a professional. All these tick boxes – because that's what my community would have looked for, for me. That's why I thought that. There was a person I met at college who was a good friend and he was quite interested in me, and I was horrified. I didn't think I would have anything but an arranged marriage at that age. And when I did consider alternatives, it was quite clear and made obvious sense to me that, 'No, things have to be done our way.' And I accepted that with some tears and tantrums. I knew nothing else. I didn't know my capacity for life and love and experience at that age. That was all I knew and those were the parameters that I had lived within so I stayed within my comfort zone. But, I feel my approach to love, sex and relationships was wholesome which I think comes from the warmth and openness I saw between my mother and father. In particular I saw my mother as a wholesome sexual being where intimacy in the home was celebrated and not concealed.

When I was younger I had visions of how married life would be but in reality it was very different and that made me a little cynical about relationships. I looked around me and most relationships were about compromise and if two people are willing to try to make it work and be respectful, it'll work. And beyond that, I never thought you could have much more than that, and I was happy to settle for that. And so I got married but I think I wasn't completely fulfilled. I didn't expect to be fulfilled! He was a serial philanderer – what can I say! It was hurtful because he was unfaithful to me, but I just thought, 'Why am I wasting my time? You're not even somebody I'd give my life for so what am I doing?' So it was easy to leave in that sense. I did work at it for a good number of years because I felt I had to, it was my duty to – I got married, I've got to make it work as best I could. When I finally left I never looked back because he wasn't the love of my life and there's no hard feelings.

I like where I'm at with my life and the situation I'm in now. I think ideally it would be nice to be with the love of my life, my soul mate, but anything less than that seems like a waste of time and I don't want to bother really. Put it this way, I feel if you're with the wrong person, it's 24/7 with the wrong person. I don't need a man to give me status, children, wealth, name, any of those things, and I don't even need a man to make me feel whole, complete. The only thing I need is tender intimacy and true companionship. There's nothing else I need, and if it's not there, then I'd rather be single and enjoy that than have to negotiate and accommodate somebody who isn't quite right.

I was once told that there are seven different levels of understanding of the Quran – the highest you'll never know. But the Quran is there for all people of all time and there are so many different ways of understanding it. And my Islam is totally different to anyone else's I know, and that's not a bad thing. That's ok because nobody else has had my experience of life, of understanding, and we all interpret within our own framework. So according to my interpretation, and I'm no Sheikh you know, wearing the hijab just stopped making sense to me. The hardest thing was, wearing hijab, my whole family had accepted me wearing the hijab. And I'd fought a lot of battles for the hijab, for women, and now I wanted to be true to my conscience but I didn't have the courage to take it off for a good number of years. It's so much harder taking it off than putting it on because of the criticism, the thinking, the questioning, the backlash of not wearing it. People are fascinated about why someone takes it off. I thought, 'Leave me alone, it's a personal decision,' but I just knew it was going to be a biggie. I was letting down the sisterhood, and I wasn't sure I could deal with that, and I was right because it felt like a lot of people took it personally.

It was a gradual process. I started justifying myself like, 'When I'm in my house I won't wear it, even if I have people round because they're my friends. These are people that I trust and I like and they should be trusting me.' These were people who were at university with me, and Muslims, part of the Islamic Society even. I was a mature student and I was married so I was a bit of a role model as well, and some girls had put on the hijab after seeing me, so can you imagine! They were inspired by me, and then to see me with it off! It was a real social responsibility, so the implications of me taking it off were huge, but I thought, 'No, I'm not wearing it in my house.'

An incident I remember when a friend came by during one of my house parties, and it was almost like I was standing there with my negligee because he didn't know where to look because I didn't have my hijab on! And I was thinking, 'This is interesting … all I've taken off is my headscarf!' And at one point he picked up a tea towel and put it on my head and said, 'That's better,' and we all had such a laugh because clearly he was uncomfortable. He was addressing the elephant in the room for the rest of the group. As time went by there were situations such as, 'I need to get milk. I'll just run across the road. I don't need it.' So I think it was a gradual process. And then when I had my children, being pregnant was almost like my hijab, because there I was with a big bump and people saw me in a different way. They saw me in a maternal way and the whole point of me wearing the hijab was so that people didn't see me in a sexual way. So I didn't really wear it consistently throughout my pregnancy, and then when I was walking around with my child, it felt like my child was my hijab. Or if I was with my husband, I felt like 'I'm with him, so it's ok.'

It's like wearing a wedding band for a lot of people. It's like, 'I've got my wedding ring on, don't approach me.' It's a bit like that. It was really difficult. It was almost like getting divorced, as I had the same reception when I got divorced, because certain women would feel threatened by me if I was talking to their husbands because I wasn't wearing hijab anymore, and then again because I wasn't married anymore. They didn't like it. They didn't like me not in hijab and I'm not even speculating. I distinctly know the difference. And I began to be excluded from certain groups. I felt this when I took off my hijab and I felt this also after my divorce, because I was perceived to have lost my status possibly, or I was a threat. Fascinating!

A couple of years ago, there was a big story in France about two girls who wanted to wear hijab and they weren't allowed to wear it in school and there was this whole debate about public and private life and expressions of faith in increasingly secular societies. At this point I'm not wearing hijab, I haven't worn it for a number of years. But it's interesting how I feel that at times I have to justify not wearing it or that I cannot support women who do choose to wear it. Now I can't remember whether it was a petition or what, but I remember sending something round, and someone emailed me back saying, "How come you're in support of these two women when you decided to take the hijab off?" and it was in an open email and I thought, 'Oh God, I've got to respond to that now!' And

so I said, "Well, the 10 years or so when I engaged with the hijab, and the journey I had, I wouldn't have missed it for the world. It was one of the most enriching experiences of my life and made me who I am today. And I would hate to think people would be deprived of that opportunity."

SELINA ULLAH
BURNING AMBITIONS

I learned that courage was not the absence of fear, but the triumph over it. The brave man is not he who does not feel afraid, but he who conquers that fear.
(Nelson Mandela)

I was born and brought up in Manchester and moved to Bradford when I was about 21. At the moment I'm the Assistant Director Safer Stronger Communities at Bradford Council. My husband and I used to live in the heart of the Asian community in Bradford 3, known as Bradford Moor, in Folkestone Street. I'd grown up in a multicultural but predominantly white inner city area – you know, a council estate – but it felt more cosmopolitan, more laid back. When we moved to Bradford we moved into quite hilly terrain where all you could see were rooftops and chimneys and concrete. It felt very claustrophobic; very tight housing, terraces and back to back houses, while in Manchester it felt more spacious.

My initial feeling about Bradford was that the contrast was very stark. It was either very white or Asian. It felt to me there wasn't anything in between. It was just a huge culture shock. The fact that unless you left the area, you could go days without seeing a white person was just – well, I couldn't comprehend it really. The area was so densely populated with Asian families – the schools, the people who lived nearby, the shopkeepers. And everything was geared around the needs of the Asian community – the shops had the Asian vegetables, fruit. And the clothes shops were fabric shops.

It was predominantly Pakistani but there were Bangladeshis there as well. You had neighbours that were very interested in your lives and I think that's cultural. But from my perspective, I wasn't used to that. The women had no barriers in terms of what they asked you – from how much you earned to what contraceptive you were using. It was almost unbelievable in terms of the lack of social barriers in some respect, because I wasn't related to them. I wasn't a friend. I was a neighbour and in terms of how I'd been brought up, there was a certain social line that you didn't cross just out of respect. But you know it was nice, and especially during the month of fasting there was a sense of belonging because at a certain time in the evening when everyone was preparing to open their fast, you could smell the cooking, frying of food and everyone you knew was geared towards the same purpose, and they were all doing the same thing at the same time. So there was a sense that the community was quite strong. But I did just miss mixing with other people, just having other interactions. It was all a very similar type of interaction and at the time I wasn't working, so for me, I was in the home most of the time and I had a three-year-old daughter so it was just the two of us, and it just felt very monocultural.

Bradford had an image even then. Being in Manchester, places like Bradford and Birmingham were always the places that had all the Asians, and we considered ourselves a bit more elite because we were a bit more mixed and we were, I suppose, 'less backward' as opposed to places like Bradford. As newcomers, our family picked up a lot of the stereotypes and a lot of the prejudices about Bradford that existed and we internalised that ourselves. Bradfordians were always seen to be very vocal about being Pakistani, being Muslims. Sometimes it was a hindrance because as Bangladeshis we just wanted to fit in. As a child, you want your world to be safe; you don't want anyone to challenge your environment or to create tensions. You don't want people to point out that you're different and you've got different needs. But I think as an adult I thought Bradford was amazingly brave, and the Pakistanis and Bangladeshis in Bradford were actually pioneering. I could appreciate that.

I actually found it really difficult to live in Bradford 3 and I moved to Keighley, which was a much smaller place. I went to live in another predominantly Asian area but that for me wasn't the issue. The issue for me was the scenery. Bradford was so concrete – roads, pavements, houses and that was it. I didn't see any green spaces. Even though I'd grown up in an inner city area in Manchester, I was used to seeing some green spaces around me. Keighley is a small town. It's much greener. It's almost like a valley and it's got hills all around it. It has a different pace. And I loved it because rather than rooftops I could see hills and I could see trees. Keighley people will always say they're from Keighley – they're not Bradfordians. And Bradford always talks about Bradford, but Keighley isn't always on the radar so there's always this tension that Keighley's been ignored or automatically assumed to be part of Bradford when in actual fact Keighley's quite distinct.

After living here for 20 years, and after having my initial culture shock and my own prejudices and so on, I think I've come a long way – I wouldn't live anywhere else now. I find Bradford and Keighley very exciting dynamic places with huge potential. The Asian community is more confident about its role and position in the Bradford district. It's like any new community. It takes a while for a community to find itself but once it does, it's able to contribute in a positive way and enhance and enrich what goes on in the district.

The booking burning of Salman Rushdie's *Satanic Verses* happened when I'd just moved to Bradford. I'm not sure if the Ray Honeyford incident was prior to that. That was the head teacher who had suggested that Asian children were holding back the learning of the white majority of children because of their inability to speak English when they came to school. There were parents protesting. It was front page news, it was television news – it was huge. It was around the time that I'd moved so I just felt, 'Where have I come to? This is going on on a daily basis!'

Then the book burning ... I think it was a shock, utter shock. The issue was that book burning was so symbolic of what had gone on in the Second World War when the Germans had burnt books, and I think the community in Bradford hadn't made that connection. I don't think they did it deliberately. You know, the people that had burnt the books hadn't realised the significance of the image and the reaction that it would create among the wider public. And I think from somebody who was standing outside, I thought, 'Did they not think? How could they not have made that connection?' So there was a bit of that, and there was almost like a, 'Do I want to be associated with something where there's that level of perceived intolerance? Why can't we have a discourse? Why can we not talk about this rather than resorting to that kind of action?' I don't know if that's because I'd been brought up in Manchester in a cosmopolitan context, where there was much more give and take, more awareness and sensitivity to others, and ways of actually trying to come to consensus about a particular position – or agreeing to disagree and leaving it at that. In contrast, in Bradford things were very cut and dry and life isn't like that.

At that point I was going home to Manchester every weekend so we had the discourse – you know, the talk, the discussions – in my mum's front room. People were saying that the protesters were mad! "Why didn't they just ignore it? It would have died anyway. They've actually put fuel to the fire because you've given them the images, you've given them the sound bites. It's a story that can run and run and run." People were a lot less media savvy in those days and I think one of the contributions that that event made was just how the media could use images and strap lines for its own benefit, and run a story for as long as it did on the basis of that. It was definitely a learning experience for a lot of people. It seems that people thought it was radical – and not in a positive way. I think being radical is generally positive – the fact that you're willing to challenge things – but this was in a negative way. The volatile response was viewed as intolerant towards other views and other perspectives and that's not what Islam's about. There was a fear that we were being portrayed in a negative way as a result of some of these actions, and these actions were emanating from Bradford. But the protests had implications for all Muslims in the UK because people won't distinguish from geography. So that's where my concern was at that time.

I hadn't heard of Islamophobia but 'Paki bashing' was a reality of my primary school years. It was there. There were skinheads and you tried to avoid them so you didn't get beaten up. Racism was something that was a national concern and it was quite high on the radar of Bradford as well. Young people encountered racism on a regular basis. There were allegations of people not getting jobs because of their background, colour and so on. There was differential treatment provided by the police with stop and search, and the perception that certain groups were being singled out for this kind of behaviour, and that was very strongly felt. And politically you had the skinheads and the National Front in those days. So all those factors were there, along with the poor economic situation of the country in the 1970s. It all fuelled anger towards other people because 'it was the fault of the other' that you're in this situation.

In the '70s and early '80s you had a lot of youth groups developing who were organised against racism and they had burning ambitions and vision that was an extremely positive motivating force, in fact we saw the politicisation of Asian youth as a whole. There was no differentiation between a Bangladeshi youth or a Pakistani or Indian youth, or whether you were a Muslim or Sikh. It was the fact that as young Asian people, they were encountering a certain type of behaviour and violence and they had to organise against that. That was a very empowering thing, which I think we've lost. It seems to me that the difficulties that our children face now – Islamophobia and continuing racism – need the same kind of collective response that we saw in the '70s and '80s. The current generation need more confidence in themselves and their potential to be constructive members of their communities.

JEAN (RABIA) YOUSFI
RAGS TO RICHES

I asked God for strength that I might achieve. I was made weak that I may learn humbly to obey. I asked for health that I might do greater things. I was given infirmity that I might do better things. I asked for riches that I might be happy. I was given poverty that I might be wise. I asked for power that I might have the praise of men. I was given weakness that I might feel the need of God. I asked for all things that I might enjoy life. I was given life that I might enjoy all things. I got nothing that I asked for, but everything that I hoped for. Almost despite myself, my unspoken prayers were answered. I am, among all men, most richly blessed. (Anon)

OUR STORIES, OUR LIVES
JEAN (RABIA) YOUSFI

I come from a quite poor working-class family background, a big family. There were seven of us; I've got three brothers and three sisters. I'm the sixth, I've got one brother younger than me. My dad was Canadian. My mum was English, from Cullingworth, really poor background; you know my mum struggled all her life. She did three jobs – she worked in the mills, she cleaned for people, she was an old people's help. My dad had mental health problems so although he worked very hard when we were younger, as he got a bit older in life he didn't really. I remember him being poorly most of the time – you know, very depressed, staying in the house all the time, not doing anything with his life and it was really hard for my mum. She really struggled.

My mum passed away when I was 13. My dad spent two years in his bedroom and then passed away as well. My mother had converted from being a Methodist to being a Catholic and she was a very very strong church goer. We were raised as quite strict Catholics. For me, it just meant we always had to go to church on Sundays and my mum tried to encourage us to pray before we went to sleep, not that any of us did that much, and just to live a good honest life really, to think about others before you think of yourself. My mother was a very generous person even though she didn't have much to be generous with. We used to be a bit amazed that my mum would give the last bowl of sugar away to the neighbours that knocked on the door, and we'd be thinking, 'What are we putting on our cornflakes in the morning?', but that was my mum.

For me growing up as a child, God was there. We prayed to him and we prayed to Jesus, and the Virgin Mary was a big player in our house. Her statues were all over the place. We even had one at the top of the steps, a little plastic statue of the Virgin Mary with a little bowl underneath it, stuck on the wall that had holy water in, and if my mum passed that, she would bless herself. Religion was my mum's thing really. It was something we did to make mum happy. When my mum did pass away I fell out with God because I couldn't get my head around why he'd taken away the one person that we needed in our lives, because dad was no good to us, and I used to say, "Why haven't you taken dad?" If there was a God that was in control of everything, then why did he do cruel things? Well, that's the way I looked at it at that time in my life.

I met my husband when I was 16. He was a student at the university, a Muslim from Algeria. He wasn't practising at the time otherwise he wouldn't have been bothering with me, would he! He'd tell me about his country, what they were allowed to do and what they weren't allowed to do, but more in a joking sense. It was as though, 'These are all the restrictions that are put upon me when I'm living back home, but now I'm living here I don't have to have these restrictions,' like we'd have a laugh and a joke about Ramadan, about them not eating at all. I realised later it was all a bit of a bravado because he did fast and he did still have his faith. I didn't know anything about Islam then and I never asked him anything about Islam. We never sat down and had conversations about religion or anything like that. Nowadays, I think a young girl meeting a Muslim boy, it would be the first point of conversation, but those days Islam to me was something that foreigners did. I was just interested in him as a person but not where he'd come from or his culture or his religious background.

I was 20 when we decided to get married. That's when we started having the conversations about his religion, once I became his wife. It's different having a girlfriend and having a wife. I think it's that once you become somebody's wife, they feel they've got some ownership over you and men feel they can then start laying down the law and tell you what you should do and shouldn't do. Once we had a child, he wanted to get back in line and be a good Muslim. So he came back to his religion, which meant that all the restrictions he was putting on himself again, he was expecting to put on me. He wanted me to be well covered up. He wanted me to stop drinking; he didn't want alcohol to be a part of our lives. Well, that was something we all did on social occasions. If my family were going out to celebrate a birthday or Christmas, they'd all have a drink, and he wouldn't want me to drink. I didn't understand why he wanted to stop me, and it would literally come to big arguments. Once I went off to my sister's birthday at the pub and I hadn't got drunk or anything. I'd only had half a glass of lager or something, just a normal English thing to do. Now when I look at it, and I think if my own son or daughter went to the pub for half a glass of lager I'd be devastated, but looking at it in those days, I thought, 'What's the big deal?' I couldn't understand why he thought it was so bad.

He wanted me to go back to live in his country and I went through six months of depression because I didn't want to go. At that time, the *News of the World* had serialised that book, *Not Without My Daughter*, about the American woman that went to Iran and she wanted to get out, but it would mean she'd have to leave her daughter behind, and I had this vision of that sort of thing happening to me when I went to Algeria to live. That he would totally change, that he would lock me in the house, that I would never be able to see my kids if I left, and just be in his control and his family's control and that was really scary. Even though it was a different country I knew that it was a Muslim country, and from meeting his sisters, I knew they didn't go out much, I knew that looking after the home was their role. I didn't really fancy doing that for the rest of my life.

But we didn't really have a future in this country. It was the time of Thatcher. We couldn't get work. So we left in 1984. I was 24. I had a big long list of rules that he had to promise me. He had to promise me that he could never tell me what to wear. He had to promise me that we would live in our own house and not live with his relatives or his mother. The third thing was that he wouldn't prevent me from leaving the house if I wanted to go out. And that he would never prevent me from coming back home if I didn't like it.

By the summer of the first year that I was in Algeria, I had decided that I wanted to look more into Islam, because I'd been very impressed at how hospitable everyone was to me, and how kind everyone was. They treated me like a princess. You know nothing was too much trouble. My favourite cake was baked every week because that was the one I liked, and they fussed over me. My sister was coming to visit me that summer, so I said, "Can you bring me a Quran," because I couldn't get one in English there. So she brought me a Quran in English and she also brought me a book – the *Sirat of the Prophet*. We spent the summer holiday together and when she left, I sat and read those two books, and they were all I read for two years. I used to read them over and over again. It was August she left, and by October I'd decided that I had to think about becoming a Muslim. The turning point for me was that I lost a child. I don't feel that now, but at the time I felt God was punishing me for not accepting the truth, even though all my relatives were saying to me, "No! God's not punishing you! This is just something that's happened." But within myself, I'd already acknowledged that Islam was the truth, but I wasn't accepting it because I knew it would put more restrictions on my life, and I felt that God didn't want me to have any more children until I became a Muslim. When I look back I don't think that was the case. I know the reason I lost the baby. I lost the baby because when I was two months pregnant, I tried to move a big packing case that we had in the backyard that was full of earth, and I got a sharp pain, and the next day I lost the pregnancy.

I felt that I'd been so far away from God for a long time, and then you feel like you have a very close personal relationship with God, and everything you do God is watching you, and everything you say God is listening to it. When I converted, I didn't know how to pray properly. I just had a few things written down on a piece of paper and I'd just go through the motions, but I prayed very deeply from within my heart to God to guide me, and to let me know if this was the right thing for me, or if this was what he wanted for me, then he had to teach me the true Islam because my in-laws didn't seem to be able to answer all my questions. And he did. He sent me lots of friends, lots of people that came to see me and started inviting me to study circles and teaching me about Islam.

We stayed there for 10 years and had to come back in 1995 because of the circumstances in Algeria – civil war. There were horrible things on the telly about whole villages being slaughtered, and we were scared we might get a knock on the door in the middle of the night. So we came back to Bradford. I had five children by then. I'd started wearing the hijab more or less straight away after becoming a Muslim, so the first time I came over here on a holiday I was wearing the hijab. I did find that a bit difficult. I was very strong with my hijab but people over here didn't understand. Like my sister didn't understand that if she was going to have the curtains wide open then I'd have to keep my scarf on all day, and she'd come home from work and I'd have closed the curtains and she'd pull them open and I'd have to go rushing off to get my scarf. And my sister's front door would be open and her friends would just knock on the door and walk straight in, and you'd have to make a beeline for the bathroom to try and find something to put on your head because you'd been sitting without a scarf on.

But the thing that I did like was that it introduced you to people you didn't know. People said salaam o alaikum if they saw you with the scarf on. One day I bumped into a sister in town who said 'salaam o alaikum' to me, and she asked, "I know all the convert sisters in Bradford. Why don't I know you?" and I explained where I lived and that. So she invited me to this big dinner. They invited me to a talk and they were very generous and gave me books and things to take home, and every time I was on holiday in Bradford, I had people I could ring up and get in touch with. So when I came back here to live, I had all these sisters here that I already knew.

Because I'm from a fashion design background, all the time I was in Algeria I was sewing clothes, day in, day out. I worked very hard when I lived over there – very elaborate ball gowns and wedding dresses I used to make, and I used to also make simple jilbabs and scarves for the Muslim sisters over there. When we came over here, we didn't know how long we were going to be over here and we had to do something until things settled down back home so we could go back. We hadn't come with the intention of staying here and bringing our children up here. And so with one of the sisters, I opened up a small Islamic clothing boutique. The shop provides an opportunity for me to talk to people, especially new sisters, because as soon as you become a Muslim, what's the first thing everyone tells you to start wearing? The hijab! So where do they come? They come and see Rabia! I sort them out with a chat and a tea and warn them about what they can expect … that they can expect racism once they start wearing hijab, that they can expect racism from Asian people because some Asian people are still racist towards white people. Even though they've become Muslims, when they walk into a room, some people will still say "gora this" or "gora that" and you know they're talking about you.

I still meet my old friends at Islamic circles – a group of like-minded Muslim sisters talking about their problems, talking about the solution to their problems and sharing tea and cakes. We try and avoid gossip because that's unIslamic, that is. I suppose non-Muslims might think of our Islamic circles as something sinister where we're building bombs and planning terrorist activities or whatever, but honestly we're more likely to be discussing what cakes we're going to cook for the next one, and swapping recipes … cake recipes, that is!

FINAL THOUGHTS

In this world women have and continue to face many challenges but as we have seen in the unfolding stories there is an incredible amount of creative leadership, talent, resourcefulness and discipline. We need to remember that we have it in us and have had it for time immemorial to be the creative spark. In doing so, we have had the experience of noting what needs changing and sustained the reflective rigour to meet the challenges that have come our way. We have sustained our energies from one generation to another and nurtured each other in the face of adversity. Such wisdom serves to engrain knowledge and open up new paths, although we can never completely know for certain where they will lead to.

Each story in *Our Stories, Our Lives* offers a mixture of both subtle and bold insights into the unique wisdom of each contributor. They show us how the seeds which were once sewn have been nurtured and grown in strength, both in the private realms of the home and in the echelons of public society. They illustrate the hopefulness and dynamism of the young and the patience, vision and experience of the old. In them we also learn from and remember the struggle of the first generation of Muslim women in Britain and many more around the world that have helped to pave a way forward in vibrant and unique ways.

The stories equally bring out into the open some of the issues that women raise. Here, there is a universal appeal in their frank and open commentary on love, marriage, motherhood; mortality, migration, racism; violence and terror as well as faith and freedom. At times humorous and always refreshing, the contributors speak passionately about concepts of global peace and justice, citizenship and belonging, education, business, entertainment and creativity; the importance of nurturing a culture of critical openness and self-discovery and more importantly the crucial role of women as architects of change.

These women encourage us to reclaim the cherished values which some may say have been eroded within a society that promotes individualism and materialism. We might live in a society where the rich get richer and the poor get poorer yet women earn 10% of world income and work two thirds of the world's working hours and hold only 14% of the world's parliamentary seats. Negara Khatun brings this message home when she speaks in the book of domestic violence as 'something that can never be justified' because 'where it exists no community can prosper'. She is right and yet domestic violence continues to be the single biggest cause of injury and death to women of any race or creed around the world. We live in a society where education is perceived to be a powerful asset in empowering us to engage in public debate, sustain human values and escape poverty. Despite the fact that young women in Britain continue to excel in education, young girls around the world are continuously denied access to education. Fatima Ayub poignantly asks us to 'question this idea of equality' because 'some are just more equal than others in this world'.

From these stories we learn that we must not underestimate the inherent power in rising to action and within these pages each woman's story reveals what is possible when we act with courage, an entrepreneurial spirit, open ourselves to faith and hold on to our sense of humour in the face of hardships. We have sustained our efforts because we believed in our capacity to alter the course of 'set paths'. We will continue to do so because we dared to believe in the realm of possibilities. With each possibility we created trajectories of responsibilities, rights and freedoms to relate to each situation (context) as it arose. While these issues will continue to dominate global agendas in years to come, at a personal level we are all more than capable of making a significant difference through our thoughts, words and actions. And in this way gently passing on our own wisdom and supporting one another to create a positive and peaceful society that continues to recognise and celebrate the massive contribution Muslim women have and continue to make both within our own communities and around the world.

Wahida Shaffi